CHOICES

CHOICES

Stop Blaming God!

CHOICES

Bill Davidson

Outskirts Press, Inc.
Denver, Colorado

CHOICES
Stop Blaming God!

Unless otherwise shown, all scripture references are taken from HOLY BIBLE INTERNATIONAL VERSION © 1973, 1978, 1984 By International Bible Societ. Used by permission of Zondervan Publishing House. All rights reserved

Outskirts Press, Inc.
http://www.outskirtspress.com

ISBN: 978-1-4327-6881-2

Outskirts Press and the "OP" logo are trademarks belonging to Outskirts Press, Inc.

PRINTED IN THE UNITED STATES OF AMERICA

Contents

Dedication & Acknowledgements

The choices I have made along the way of life have sometimes affected my wife Jean more than they have me, so my first thanks go to her, who for almost fifty years has put up with me, whether my choices proved to be right or wrong.... and I'll leave the reader to guess which predominated.

Our children, Kellie, Craig and John, are all adults now, living their own lives. Their foundational years were dependant on the choices we made, which often took them from certain securities into risky living. But I doubt they would have had it any other way. To Kellie, I give extra thanks for wading through these pages before they were published. She has proved to be the excellent teacher I never had as a child.

For many years now my church family in Church of The Nations, Lake Luzerne, and Church of The King in Queensbury, has surrounded us with faithfulness, support, correction and love, for which I am wholeheartedly grateful.

My extended family in Alliance International Ministries, especially the Coordinating Teams on which I serve, here in the States, in Australasia, South America and West Africa, are a safe place for me and mine. I thank them for being such an example of the true and selfless Body of Christ.

In these pages I make mention of The Salvation Army, the good and faithful basis of my early life, and Youth With a Mission, where leaders and teachers took the straggled edges of my belief and experience and wove them together into much of what you will read here.

Whether or not you take this work and reach its closing pages, I am satisfied that I have expressed the ideas in this book. In the midst of your busyness, whether you read on, or set it aside, is one of your many choices.

Bill Davidson
Queensbury, New York.

1

Choices, Choices!

THIS IS A book about choices, those actions of the will that set the course of our lives and shape our destiny. Some choices we make by our own devices, while others, especially when we are children, are made for us.

Later in this book we'll wade into some theology along the way, so let's start gently...

Sitting in Mr. Mackintosh's classroom in St. George's Primary School in Bromley, Kent, there wasn't a cloud in my ten year old sky. The calendar was approaching the mid 1950s. Unlike our American counterparts, we made no pretence at silly 'duck and cover' exercises to prevent atomic bombs from landing on our heads. England knew that this would have been a laughable response to the Doodlebugs - Hitler's rocket bombs in the last months of the war - never mind the mega tonnage of an Atomic Bomb. Nor did we think there was a 'Commie' under every bed or around every corner. Our society had just about picked up the pieces left over from the Second World War which had ended just nine years before, and we weren't looking for another fight. Not right now, thank you!

Only a few years before, Britain and its populace had been classified as being below starvation level, so the advent of the peaceful Fifties gave some signs of hope and stability.

Although we didn't know it at the time, our vast British Empire was fading fast. Just as well, really. Had it continued there would have been a noticeable shortage of pink ink in all the cartographers' offices, because in those days vast reaches of the known world from northern Canada to New Zealand were suitably shaded thus as 'British'. I admit to feeling quite sorry for all the other bits which looked neglected and lonely outside the beneficent pink of our far-flung empire on which the sun never set! That, I think, was as close as we came to actual racism. Although we had never actually met any, all the black and brown people of which we were aware were British, anyway. Or so we thought in our smug little society.

In my previous hometown of Sheffield, the home of Britain's steel industry, my friends and I had played on bomb sites; those missing teeth in rows of houses where some family had once resided but which now lay wasted, bare and open. But Bromley was not scarred in any way. Although now a suburb of Greater London, Bromley was then a peaceful Kentish town with little shops on the main street, ending with Vic's Music Store, which sported a Davy Crocket hat in the window to advertize the latest 'hit' record. A hat, I might add, which became mine, thanks to my sister Helen who worked there – or rather, thanks to Victor, the owner, who had an eye for my sister. It didn't do him much good; she looked elsewhere. Maybe he should have given me a copy of the record as well as the hat and I might have put in a good word for him. As it was I was a bit disgusted with that hat. On closer inspection, I discovered that it had "Davey Crocket" written on the brown material on the top and I knew from experience - having seen actual photos from the film - that the real Mr. Crocket did NOT have his name written across the top of his head! Fake!

Now back to that classroom. I cannot recall much of what we learned there. I just remember slow sunny walks home with Janet Green and Elizabeth Grey, the first two girls for whom I fell for at around the age of eight. That was until they introduced me to my first great love, Donna Blum. She was a blonde from Dayton, Ohio, and her father, a US Air Force Colonel, had a 'Yank Tank', a car fully three times longer than any British automobile and twice the width. It had wings out the back and was colored turquoise, no less! When its trunk was open - which we called a 'boot' - it sat six or seven of us comfortably, with our legs dangling over the back bumper. Donna let me try her 'pogo stick', a thing of mystery to all us Bromley-ites, and then asked me in for cookies. Another mystery until I found they were just like English 'biscuits', not bought in a shop but actually made at home by a Mom who looked like the lady from 'Leave it to Beaver'!

Now I *must* get back to that classroom. I was ten years old and sitting in the second row from the right hand side. On the far right sat the 'older children' who were about to take their 'Eleven Plus' examination which, by whether they passed or failed, determined if they would go to a good school or be relegated to a 'Secondary Modern', after which they would work in a shop or as a laborer. In the good school they would all 'talk proper' and wear blazers and caps with a coat of arms on each, whereas in the other school they would all 'talk common' and wear whatever they wanted.

My peaceful world was interrupted by the entry of Miss Varley, a stern but sweet lady with kindly eyes and an upper crust accent. The world in which I grew up was classified, you see, by accents, which identified not only from whence you came - in some parts of England to within a mile or so - but also from what 'class' of people into which you were born. Miss Varley was our Head Mistress, the English equivalent of a Principal.

"Attention children," she warbled. "The Eleven Plus examination is next week and we congratulate all our top form and wish them jolly good luck!" We all concurred and gave them three cheers, "Hip, Hip…." Etcetera.

It was then that a thunderbolt struck the school. Miss Varley muttered something to Mr. Mackintosh and then announced, "We've decided to put William in with the Eleven Plus children, so he will also be taking the examination at the same time." I think she may have added something else, something about that being a splendid idea because I had done so well, but a blur entered my vision and my hearing, and both at the same time. From that moment on all I heard was something like that trombone sound that Charlie Brown hears whenever his teacher is talking.

Later that day my parents were informed and of course they were duly honored, delighted, and humbled, along with several other expressions of parental pride with which they were probably bursting. Had they been old enough to understand what was really happening, no doubt my sisters would have been amused at the idea of their silly little brother being put into a classification with children fully eighteen months to two years ahead of his own. So far as they were concerned it was just a short while ago they had finished teaching me to tie my shoes. So far as I was concerned I was convinced that this was a big mistake. Here was I whose only credentials in life were that I knew how to play the drums, how to play most brass band instruments, was conversant with all the words to 'Davey Crocket', and fairly regularly was known to fall in love.

Somehow I scraped through the Eleven Plus, but I had a feeling that I didn't belong in that exam room, and when I was selected to an interview at our number one school choice I knew I was doomed. The interview consisted of twenty minutes of mind-numbing terror as two men in black academic gowns asked me questions. So far as I was concerned they might have been speaking Mandarin, to which I replied in Portuguese – it was that bad. I left the room feeling absolutely humiliated.

"Oh, my Lord!" my mother exclaimed. "You look as if you've seen a ghost!" Indeed I was a whiter shade of pale as I exited the failed interview. The shame and futility of it all crowded in on my little life.

Incredibly (to me at least) I still made it into one of the 'nice' schools;

the type where you wore the blazer and cap and called everybody 'Sir', whatever their gender. But then came Liverpool.

At the age of twelve I left the languid fields of Kent and moved to Merseyside where everything was black with the soot from a million small houses belching coal smoke from broken chimney pots. They still had bomb sites in Liverpool, but it didn't make much difference because the whole place looked like one in those days. As to my school – if you could call it that – it was a decaying pile. Had I been a movie director and needed a location for Oliver Twist, our school would have been just right, although some might have thought we were overdoing the drabness a bit! It was a crumbling old relic of Dickensian days, but that wasn't the end of my culture shock.

I was part of a class of about thirty-five lads who, after I learned their language - which took about two weeks of hard study and imitation - turned out to be among the funniest and liveliest people I have ever met, anywhere. Humor had not been a pronounced part of life in Kent, but in Liverpool it was a religion.

Our main expression of this skill was to 'ave a laff' in school. This took the form of singing out loud while a troubled faculty member would sit, frustrated but helpless, at his desk. And when I say 'sing' I mean *really sing*.

We had a repertoire of Orange Lodge songs, all anti-Catholic, composed by members of the Lodge that to this day celebrates the Protestant Victory of "King Billy" over Catholic Ireland on July 12th, 1690! The irony was that at least half the boys were Catholics, but hardly religious enough to realize that the lines about 'kicking the Pope' had any theological or ecclesiastical significance. As we sang, we drummed on our desks to our sheer delight. It sounded great, and I couldn't believe my good fortune in escaping my academic mis-givings. Anything remotely academic would have been sorely out of place in this school. I had found my home!

Only once or twice did a staff member fight back and take the lot of us downstairs to be caned. Two whacks with a three-quarter-inch wide and four-foot long cane administered with full force, leaving two parallel blue lines on the buttocks – two for each whack. After my first swipe, I straightened up in surprise. I had never imagined anything so painful!

"Bend over again" said Mr. Tueland, the Math teacher. "I said 'two'." "Oh, please sir," I whimpered, Oliver Twist-like, but definitely not asking for 'more'.

"Oh, alright Davidson. Off you go." He muttered something about me being a good Salvation Army boy. His Catholic guilt must have risen up in that moment as he clutched the cane in one hand and his Rosary in the other. I thanked him and briefly repented of my Protestant leanings!

But it made no difference. We were roundly cheered by the rest of the school as we marched, single file, back to the classroom, where our chorus continued, with the addition of some ribald verses learned from one or two students who had brothers in the Merchant Navy – a good cop-out for lads from Liverpool. One of my abiding fears is that in my senility I might regale my family with a few of these ditties! However 'sanctified' I may have become; I remember every word to this day!

Up to that point it was the choices of teachers and parents that steered me, but in my early teens I made a choice that could have cost my life. Jeffrey Hulbert suggested that Wally Waters and I should join him in climbing the new ten-storey apartments on Everton Hill. He had heard there was a great view of The Mersey from the roof.

The fact that we had seen the Mersey up close didn't seem to matter. It actually sounded quite sane, that is until we got to the outside corridor running past the apartment doors on the tenth floor. To get to the roof from there we had to stand on the outside half-wall, catch hold of the overhanging roof and pull ourselves up onto the roof it-self. Jeffrey and I did this with little bother and even less sense. Wally stayed on terra firma.

The police were called within minutes. We were hauled down by a worried group of tenants and a furious constable and taken back to school in the Paddy Wagon, so named because it was usually on duty to pick up inebriated Irishmen from the streets of Liverpool and take them to the local lock-up to dry out. As we dismounted the dark blue vehicle, the entire school crowded the windows and cheered like a football crowd as Hulbert, Davidson and Waters filed out and on their way to a good hiding. For me, however, it meant that the kid from Kent was now accepted – one o' d' lads! A wacker! [1]

In time the feelings of academic inferiority slipped from my shoulders. No-one in this hell-hole of a school cared about academics. We were there for a laugh and the only serious business was the study of the one great religion of the city – football. It is common knowledge in that city that there are four great Cathedrals in Liverpool; the modern Catholic Cathedral, designed rather like a cone, so the locals call it The Mersey Funnel (to rhyme with the Mersey Tunnel that runs under the famous river). The second is the Anglican Cathedral, still modern but more classical in its lines. Then there are the two great and best at-tended centers of worship, Anfield and Goodison Park, the homes of Liverpool and Everton football clubs. It was to the science celebrated at these two shrines we gave our full and rapt attention.

I look back now and see how certain choices - some made for me by those around me and others which I took myself - formed a place for me in society and an identity which was far less than that for which I was born. Subsequent choices taken later in life often sprang from the attitudes formed by those earliest decisions. Choices change lives.

---

1   Wacker – pronounced: *wach-ah – (as in achtung)* a trustworthy companion, a mate.

2 | Choosing Failure

I HAVE OFTEN witnessed it; people who fear responsibility, or who have come to the conclusion that their lives won't measure up, purposely – although often unconsciously – choose to fail.

There are many effective ways of doing this. Sometimes plans are made which are so impractical or grandiose that they will obviously fail. The subsequent failure takes place, to the sub-conscious relief of the planner. Other people self-destruct through some outrageous behavior just before success might have arrived, just in case it decides not to.

There's an interesting verse in Ecclesiastes. It says *"Do not let your mouth cause your flesh to sin, nor say before the messenger of God that it was an error. Why should God be angry at your excuse and destroy the work of your hands?"* [2] One translation of that word *'messenger'* is *'angel'*. It reminds me of the time Daniel was resolutely set on a course of action, and prayed for wisdom and understanding. Eventually an angel appeared and said *"Since the first day that you set your mind to gain understanding and to humble yourself before your God, your words were heard, and I have come in response to them. But the prince of the Persian kingdom resisted me twenty-one days."* [3]

---

2   Ecclesiastes 5:6,7 (NKJV)
3   Daniel 10:12,13

It took three weeks for the answer to turn up, during which time Daniel chose to remain resolute and in faith. But what if he had begun to doubt and choose to behave badly? Would the verses in Ecclesiastes have come to life? [4]

My elementary school 'promotion', before my time, into a class for which I was not prepared, touched something deep inside me that influenced not only the rest of my school days, but also the first thirty years of my life. It's still a fight to this day, another thirty years on. It was a lie that told me I would never make it. Once that lie had invaded my soul I consistently chose to take the path of least resistance, never again to allow that humiliating blush of failure.

My father would have never believed this, but much of my boyhood was spent with the conscious thought that I would never measure up to him. I surpassed him in height by the time I was fourteen but there was much more to my Dad than his physical stature, which never amounted to much. I remember him speaking to one of his colleagues about me as I stood close by. They commented about my success and ministry. "We sit at his feet" my Dad said. I was shocked, mostly because I had never heard my father say anything which I thought of as a gross exaggeration. He was my giant. How could I ever measure up?

My school in Liverpool did nothing to refute this lie of self doubt; it only allowed it to remain unchallenged. One day, at the age of fifteen, I walked out the back door. I had 'graduated', in the American sense, by remaining on the premises long enough to quit, legally. No ceremonies were ever held, for me or any other student. I had 'stayed on' to try for some further exams to gain a qualification of sorts, but I left before facing yet more humiliation, joking my way through life on the outside but forlorn and hopeless within.

Later, at a college level, an educational diagnostician sat with me, attempting to assess my abilities. My lack of any formal qualifications

---

4   More of this great story of Daniel in the chapter 'Star Wars of Darkness & Light'

suggested that I should begin in the lowest possible class, where I sat with one student who was learning to read. We were instructed in Bible by a sweet elderly lady who reminded me more of a children's Sunday School teacher than a college professor. In her Welsh brogue she would read the stories of Jesus and end with, "Isn't that lovely now?" And from her, it was.

John Larsson, only a few years older than I and who later became the international leader of The Salvation Army, invited me to sit with him as he studied early each morning. He presented me with a small booklet, "An Introduction to Theology". Although I was an avid reader, mostly of Shakespeare and Dickens, I hardly knew how to approach actual study. His generous attempts – although falling on potentially good soil – came well before planting season.

Seemingly the educational expert saw more potential than was evident in my record. I took some aptitude and intelligence tests and, in a follow-up interview, he smiled (a rarity with this man) and said, "I just want to find out if you're a genius or just playing around with us." Obviously he was joking and I had my own ideas about which of those it might be, so I just laughed in what I hoped was an intelligent and sophisticated manner. That usually seemed to work. Seemingly the tests had shown an ability to think 'laterally' and 'outside the box'. Unfortunately I wasn't even aware of the box's existence.

It took me the entire length of my college days to be promoted, step by step, through three levels, to the top class, where I sat, ridiculously awed by those around me, for the last two classes before graduation.

Years later, in my thirties, after I experienced a release of the power of the Holy Spirit in my life,[5] I chose to challenge that old sense of inferiority by studying for my Bachelor's degree in Theology, followed by a Masters in Divinity, and finally my doctorate. At every step I felt I must be cheating. It all seemed too easy. Whenever I received work back with glowing responses I re-checked the name on the front. It

---

5   You'll read more about the process of this experience in Chapter 12

had to be someone else's paper! But no, it was me, but me now free of the old patterns, old feelings, and old habits.

I have since learned that a habit is merely a choice that has gained momentum!

Please don't imagine that my childhood was a sad affair. My teenage years were great fun. But surrounding that enjoyment was a pattern of behavior based on an avoidance of having to personally choose anything which might have shown me up for what I had begun to believe myself to be; a failure. That is not to suggest that I had a life devoid of challenge. God arranged things to ensure that I always had more than my fair share of responsibility, and He continues to do so.

It didn't help much that my academic short-comings were hardly noticeable due to some other attributes which often proved as useful as any university education, or more so. My abilities with humor, music, writing and drama, and an ability to 'play the part' won me some prominence and no little success during my early years of ministry. [6] It also helped to be in an organization in which 'name and fame' played a major role in one's recognition and progress, often irrespective of spiritual maturity or character, and those years were blessed (or cursed) with both name and fame.

The specter of failure and inadequacy influenced many of my choices and corrupted what God might have had for me in earlier years. How many times did I unconsciously choose how to win acceptance for myself in personal relationships, or recognition and affirmation in ministry, solely on the basis of feeding my deep sense of lack, which all began with a choice, somewhere in childhood? Now I can look back and identify this struggle, but at the time I was completely unaware that such issues even existed.

I remember standing on the stage of The Royal Albert Hall singing one of my favorite songs, Joy Webb's "There Will be God". Twelve thou-

---

6   More of this in 'Marked for Life' by Bill Davidson

sand people packed the place. As the classical introduction began you could have heard a pin drop.

> Ten thousand worlds may pass away
> And bring the dawning of a cosmic day
> Age after age – time after time
> Hold its sway

I had sung it dozens of times before, all over the UK and in some of the greatest concert halls of Europe and Scandinavia. This time it seemed different.

> Man walks alone amid uncertainty
> Only one thing can still make him strong
> In the doubt, in the fear, in the loneliness
> In the struggle of right against wrong

The rest of The Joystrings had been supplanted by a string quartet. Joy was on the Grand Piano and one thousand voices lined the choir stall behind us. Brindley Boon, a master composer and renowned musician, conducted. I stood alone, out front. To be truthful I was in my element as we brought the powerful song to its conclusion.

> In the doubt, in the fear, in the loneliness
> In the struggle of right against wrong
> Somewhere, amidst the confusion
> There will be hope, there will be love
> There will be God!

The choir echoed the last line with the dramatic rallentando: "There.. will.. be... GOD!"

I knew the applause would be deafening, and it was. Salvationists recognize great music when they hear it, but even more they love music that recognizes God's greatness. In this song Joy had not wasted a word or a note.

There is no sound quite like the applause of a large crowd and as it rose from the bowels of that massive concert hall I ran from the stage. Joy followed me and we sprinted halfway around the back corridor of the Albert Hall, only stopping to wonder what we were doing. "They're still clapping!" Joy said. But it was too late to re-enter, and it felt inappropriate. It would have looked too much like a 'concert curtain call'. This moment seemed too sacred for such show.

I regret now that I did not stay on stage to enjoy God receiving His applause. I – you see – was struggling with my secret hunger for affirmation and recognition, and somehow I knew I should be out of the picture at that great moment.

The evening was being recorded by EMI and was published as an album. The producer, one of the EMI men who looked after The Joystrings when we visited the Abbey Road studios, told me some time later that a leader in The Salvation Army, who was responsible for some aspects of Army music, had stood by him throughout our rendition, laughing and mocking as I sang. He didn't much like the contemporary way we treated our performances and would have preferred... well; I'm not sure who or what! As the song concluded and the crowd responded with thunderous applause, the EMI producer turned to this man beside him and said, "If you don't want that song on the record, then so far as EMI is concerned you haven't got a record!"

At the time I knew nothing of this, but I knew something of the intense criticism which was leveled at us for choosing to be pioneers of contemporary Christian music. Brindley Boon himself told me, some forty years later, that he had kept much of that criticism from those of us in the group because it was so hurtful.

Perhaps, that night, I caught something of the spiritual warfare which was taking place in the Heavenlies. Maybe the conflict between pride and humility in my own heart only reflected the competition in the Heavens, which also reared its head in the constant striving for 'excellence' among Salvation Army musicians. In my own soul, the conflict continued.

Part of life and maturity is taking stock of one's existence through the perspective of age and experience. So much was lost in those years, all because of a lie from the enemy of God's people and a few sincere but poor choices along the way. To this day I am hesitant when I see parents glowing with pride at the idea of their children being pushed ahead and promoted, and I pray that it is for the best. For some it is a genuine step in the right direction.

It happened in the opposite direction for me too, when I was not pushed ahead, but held back. At one point in my teens it was suggested that I attend the Royal Academy of Dramatic Arts, but it was decided, on my behalf, that this was no place for a nice Christian boy. Knowing me, at that time, I think Mum was probably right!

I have decided that regret is the worst of all uses of time and energy, and I will never allow it to cloud my vision. God is a God of restored years. The choices I have made along the way have still proved to be the sort of stuff that God can accept and turn into an amazing life-experience.

It is intriguing to play the 'what if' game. What if the Confederacy had won the Civil War? What if Hitler had decided to take the short hop across the twenty-miles of the English Channel instead of turning to invade his Soviet allies a thousand frozen miles to the east? What if I had not gone to Sunbury Court at the age of fourteen and had never met my Jean? What if she had decided not to attend the Joystrings concert seven years later, when visiting her brother in Manchester? What if I had simply said 'Hello' to her after the concert, handed her an autograph and walked away? What if we had decided to remain within the safety net of The Salvation Army? What if I had never become desperate enough to cry out to God for the power of His Spirit? What if we had never stepped out in faith and.....?

I cannot say that I would not have chosen differently, had I the opportunity, but I can say that had I taken a different path I would still want to end up where I am today! As I write, I am sitting in Monrovia,

Liberia, in the house of my friends Philipson and Victoria Nagbe. Jean, for her part, is leading a ladies' team to Bogotá, Colombia. In a few days we will be back in New York to celebrate Thanksgiving with three generations of our loving family – that's typical of our adventurous life!

It seems that my choices, good or bad, were not the only determining factor in my life, but to understand that, you'll have to read on.

3

St. Bertram the Blamed

IN EVERY TOWN throughout the world a statue should be erected. We could call him St. Bertram, or more fully, "St Bertram the Blamed". I have chosen his name randomly on the basis of alliteration alone, so my Bertram should not be confused with any other Bertram of history, sainted or otherwise. Our St. Bertram is simply created to meet our universal need to blame someone. We could blame Bertie for… well, for everything!

How convenient it would be if we could 'Blame Bertie' when, on our way to an important meeting, we get stuck behind an agricultural vehicle, the main aim of which seems to be to get to its destination sometime before next September.

When we turn up to church twenty minutes late, rather than slink to our seats covered in guilt, we could hold our heads high as we acknowledge the sympathetic smiles of all around. After all, Bertie was to blame for our tardiness.

Sloppy work, bad decisions, broken relationships, unpaid bills and all the ill-timed impulse buying which maxed-out our credit cards, could all be laid at the feet of Bertram. We could have an annual *Blame Bertram Day* during which the entire nation could breathe a collective sigh of relief as all responsibility for mishaps and mayhem could be cast at the feet of our favorite saint.

On the other hand, perhaps Bertie the Blamed is already redundant. Haven't we filled his role with other targets of blame, such as 'Someone Else', or 'The Devil' or even 'God' Himself?

When it comes to how and why things happen, we humans have a great capacity for living in denial. It's so much easier if we can shift the blame from ourselves and onto our circumstances or some other power beyond our control. Whatever happens in life, we always plead "extenuating circumstances". We have cultivated the idea that personal responsibility is an ill-fitting coat which too heavily burdens our peace of mind.

Getting back to God and the Devil, they have each carried an unreasonable load of blame throughout human history. But wait, you say, surely the Devil is behind all wrong-doing, isn't he? Well, he is certainly the tempter, but temptation is an influence, not a cause. It's far too easy to say, "The Devil made me do it".

Have you ever been confronted by a well meaning Christian who says something like this: "I was running late, got held up in traffic and then just as I pulled onto the freeway on the way to church, I ran out of gas. Then I realized I'd left my wallet at home. I had no gas can in the car and I had to walk a mile in the rain. Of course, wouldn't you know, I had no raincoat with me."

No great theological problem so far, but then he closes with this one: "The Devil's really taking his shots at me. I must be doing something right! Right?"

It's all too easy to respond with an "Amen, brother!" when what is really needed is, "You idiot! What were you playing at?"

It sounds so spiritual, this picture of the struggling saint valiantly making his martyred way to church against all odds and under attack from the Enemy. But reality is somewhere else on the spiritual scale. Obviously he had not planned his day well. Other priorities had taken the place of preparing himself, spirit, soul and body, for going to meet with his fellow believers. Being ready to worship his God was obviously far from his mind or else he would not have forgotten to put gas in his tank. Moreover, what was he doing, coming to a church service without money in his pocket! And isn't it a bit prideful to think that the Devil himself has him targeted because he is such a danger to the principalities of darkness? More often than not, people who are "doing something right" are *less* likely to be under attack from the enemy, not more.

Blaming Satan for your every difficulty presupposes that he even knows where you are and what you are doing, as if he is omnipresent, [7] and omniscient. [8]

Job tells us that God once asked Satan where he had been and where had he come from. Satan replied, *"From roaming through the earth and going back and forth in it."* [9] That "back and forth" is a tell-tale testimony of a being limited in time and space. When he was back, he was back and when he was forth, he was forth, and when he was only halfway back he was neither back nor forth!

So let's stop handing out accolades to Satan when at least half the time he has contributed little or nothing to our challenging circumstances. He does enough harm without being given the glory for every slip twixt cup and lip!

However, we know Satan is not alone. He has a myriad of disobedient angels who have turned into demons. They can communicate up-line through their various demonic networks, all the way to the Prince of Darkness himself, but they are all liars, just as Satan himself

---

7   Omnipresent – being present everywhere
8   Omniscient - having complete or unlimited knowledge, awareness, or understanding; perceiving all things.
9   Job 1:7

"was a liar from the beginning".[10] So imagine the chaos in their communications department, with every demon at every level passing along a slightly corrupted version of what the reality actually is!

But we still have the other alternative – to blame God. Surely He is the Author of all things. He's in control, isn't He? Can anything happen outside of His will?

Consider the outburst from a Steve Johnson, a wideout for the Buffalo Bills, after dropping a game-winning pass. For those of you who live outside the United States this means that Steve is paid mega-bucks to run several yards and then catch a ball. Now, I realize that this is something most of us learn around the age of three, but it's not as easy as it sounds, especially when someone else is running beside you, trying to intercept the ball or at least knock it to the ground. And then they make you wear a helmet which blocks your peripheral vision. But as they say, 'it's not rocket science' and on the day in question there wasn't anyone within several yards of Mr. Johnson.

The basics are as follows: you see the ball coming, expertly delivered from another millionaire on your team whose job it is to throw the ball to you, and then you catch it. For these skills you can become a national hero or, on the other hand, a national let-down if you happen to fail in this basic but precise science. It's not fair, but that's why you get paid the big bucks.

On a crisp November day in 2010 the Buffalo Bills were facing the superior Pittsburg Steelers. A tied game led into overtime and only a few minutes remained, when it happened. The Quarterback, Ryan Fitzpatrick, delivered a perfect pass, spiraling through the air to drop conveniently over the shoulder of Johnson and into his waiting arms. It would have been difficult to deliver a baby more efficiently. For his part, Johnson was already in the end zone when the delivery arrived. Six game-winning points, here we come! The problem was that Steve

---

10   John 8:44

watched in horror as the ball continued past his outstretched arms, through his hands, and on to the ground. Incomplete!

The Steelers compounded this regrettable but unforgettable moment by getting the ball back and winning the game with a last minute field goal.

This epic moment in US History is not the point of the story! What came next is my point. Before the young man had even made the journey home – which might have given him a little more time to consider his next move - he lashed out on his I Pad via Twitter at the one person who was obviously to blame. Not his coach for calling the game-winning play, or Fitzpatrick for neatly delivering the game winning pass, nor himself for dropping this opportunity to become a hero. No, he blamed God. Here's his Tweet: *"I praise you 24/7!!!!! And this is how you do me" "You expect me to learn from this??? I will never forget this!! Ever!!! Thx…"*

Perhaps he withdrew his hostile response to the heavens in time. After all, the fault can be placed elsewhere. There's always Satan… or St. Bertram… his Pop Warner coach… his Mom…his Third Grade teacher… anyone, in other words, but the guy who dropped the ball.

Believers who would not dare to blame God still wallow in some murky waters when times get tough. Don't we regularly suffer the most atrocious experiences and bring ourselves some form of cruel comfort by trotting out horrendous statements, such as: "Everything happens for a purpose", and "God is just testing us to draw us closer to Him."

I cannot count the times I've heard someone pour out a testimony of mishaps, mistakes, mess-ups and maladies, only to finish with, "I just don't know what God is doing!" As if the Almighty would set these catastrophes in motion, like traps along our pathway, and all in order to "draw us closer to Him"! Consider the ridiculous concept of Almighty God sitting somewhere in the dim and distant past, proclaiming; *"And behold, even though thou praise me and even though thou wilt promise to do a Jesus dance in the end zone with forefingers raised to the Heavens, lo, I will cause thee to drop the ball and look like an overpaid idiot, for thus I have decreed in my wisdom before the foundation of the world."* Surely we can't accept that image of God, unless of course you're a Steelers fan and delighted in Steve's momentary downfall!

Perhaps the young footballer had never understood the words of James, when he wrote, *"When tempted, no one should say, 'God is tempting me.' For God cannot be tempted by evil, nor does he tempt anyone; but each one is tempted when, by his own evil desire, he is dragged away and enticed. Then, after desire has conceived, it gives birth to sin; and sin, when it is full-grown, gives birth to death."* [11]

Consider the awful day in January 2011 when Representative Gabrielle Giffords was shot in Tucson, Arizona. Several bystanders were injured and others slain, including a sweet nine-year-old girl. In the midst of such tragedy we would all search our hearts for any suitable response. To explain such sin is beyond us. But when one young spokesman was interviewed on camera, he said, "We must all just say that every-thing happens for a reason." Others spoke of the need to accept God's will, as if He had planned this hideous moment for some purpose of His own making!

It is understandable for people under stress to reach out for any form of comfort, but platitudes and clichés might bring solace in the mo-ment, but only truth heals.

The old song said: *"To added affliction He addeth His mercy, to mul-tiplied trials, He multiplies peace."* [12] That, my friend, is what God is doing. The god who plans catastrophes for his followers, just to attract them to a closer walk with him is hardly the same deity! And would you honestly want to spend eternity with this author of mischief?

---

11   James 1:13-15
12 ' He Giveth More Grace' by Annie J Flint (1866-1932)

There must be other reasons for our dilemmas and disasters, our trials and tribulations – and there are. They are called 'Choices', the actions of our will.

This book can become a discovery, a revelation of your Will; that powerhouse that drives every choice and fires every action. Ultimately, the consequences of our choices will be the only things for which we will be judged, so it is profoundly important that you read on. But let me make it clear – you don't have to continue... That's up to you. It's your choice...

4

Freedom!

WE WERE NOT the first beings ever made, nor were we the first animate moral beings God chose to create. More of what that means, later. We are, however, quite different from all others. The Bible states, *"Then God said, 'Let us make man in our image, in our likeness.'"* [13] What does that mean? It certainly doesn't mean that we are divine, nor will we ever become so. The Bible makes that clear, despite the blasphemous claim of Brigham Young, the founder of the Mormons, who said "as we are, God once was, and as God is, we will one day be."

God's phrase "in our likeness" means a great deal when we begin to understand what God is like? It's an important question because everyone has an opinion, from truth to silly fiction, from heresy to convenient compromise.

It's impossible for us to get to know God on our own terms and by our own intellectual endeavor. How can the finite – those who are limited in dimension – discover Him who is infinite unless of course He has chosen to reveal Himself? Fortunately God has done a more-than-adequate job of that.

For instance, God has revealed Himself through that which He has

13 Genesis 1:26

made. The Creation shows qualities of the Creator. Despite the fact that Stephen Hawking's prodigious intellect concluded in his latest book, *"Because there is a law such as gravity, the universe can and will create itself from nothing."* He goes on to claim, *"It is not necessary to invoke God to light the blue touch paper and set the Universe going."* [14]

It boggles my less-than-prodigious intellect to note the nonsense in that statement. Can Hawking be implying that we should believe that a law such as gravity can be classified as 'nothing'? Where did the law come from? Who or what set it in place? Can a law exist outside of intelligence? 'Nothing' implies the existence of 'no-thing', including the energy involved in a gravitational effect and the law that defines its abilities.

Sorry, Prof., you'll have to dig deeper before dismissing the existence of the eternal - and there has to be an eternal entity of some sort, or else we are left with that quandary of absolutely nothing becoming positively something, a quandary with which Professor Hawking has yet to successfully grapple.

God has also revealed Himself through His Word, the Bible - an amazing and lively declaration of His character and purposes. Then God has chosen to reveal Himself through his dealings with the nation Israel. It must seem a heavy burden at times to realize that the whole point of their existence as a people is for God to show Himself through them, to the nations.

In like manner, God has chosen to reveal Himself through the Church. As a Christian it's exciting to read the words, *"His intent was that now, through the church, the manifold wisdom of God should be made known,"* [15] and *"God placed all things under his feet and appointed him to be head over everything for the church, which is his body, the fullness of Him who fills everything in every way."* [16]

14   The Grand Design' by Stephen Hawking & Leonard Mlodinow – Bantom Books 2010
15   Ephesians 3:9,10
16   Ephesians 1:22,23

God's greatest revelation is, of course, embodied in His decision to become *incarnate* and live among us. The apostle John says, *"The Word became flesh and made his dwelling among us. We have seen his glory, the glory of the One and Only, who came from the Father, full of grace and truth."* [17] What this greatest revelation shows us is that God is a relational being. Consider the fact that Jesus teaches us to look on the awesomeness of God and call Him 'Father', in fact, to call Him 'Abba'… Daddy!

We also discover something of God's heart when we watch how Jesus, the Son, related to His Father and we see, revealed to the simplest of us, the amazing qualities of relationship within the Trinity.

We can only understand relationship from the context of separation. From the moment our umbilical cord is cut, and for the rest of our lives, we must struggle with relating to others across the divide of separateness. God has never known such an interruption in His relationship within the Trinity Godhead. He has enjoyed perfect unity and oneness; perfect relationship.

When the Word of God describes Him it states, *"The Lord our God is one Lord."* [18] That word 'one', properly translated, means 'united'. [19] So we see that God has enjoyed relationships and for eternity-past has participated in a holy, complete and unbroken relational oneness.

At this point, it's important to get one thing straight. God does not need us for relationship! Years ago I heard a preacher on the radio say, "God was lonely, so He created mankind." I would not mention it but for the fact that I've heard it repeated over the years. That idea belongs in the same tub as the liquid they use to wash the hogs! God doesn't need us! He has *chosen* to create us and has placed within us the attributes necessary to actually join in His pre-existing relationships! Amazing!

---

17 John 1:14
18 Deuteronomy 6:4 (KJV)
19 Strong's OT: 259 'echad' - a numeral from OT:258; united, (New Exhaustive Strong's Numbers and Concordance with Expanded Greek-Hebrew Dictionary. Copyright © 1994, 2003).

In order to grant us these attributes which make up this wonderful capacity to relate, God took what we might think was an almighty risk; He set His humans entirely and totally free, because He knew there was no such thing as a meaningful relationship without it being in the context of absolute freedom of choice.

God also understands that no quality of character can be formed without that same freedom. Choice is at the root of everything worthwhile, but it can also be the doorway to every form of foolishness. Choice, unhindered, unfettered, without manipulation or control, is the hub of relationship.

So, what was the risk? Well, if God were to set mankind free, the likelihood of wrong choices must be allowed. In fact it's not a risk, more a predictable conclusion. Rebellion will, sooner or later, take to the streets and ruin the relationship. You might ask "Then why bother? Why not simply create beings who would stay 'in love' with God, continually obedient to Him?" But if they are your questions, then you don't yet know what love is, or even what it means to be obedient!

Allow me to ask you a question. What qualities should a single person look for in a potential marriage partner? Hopefully this 'single' has greater discernment than Samson who, when Delilah had captured his attention, told his parents, *"Get her for me. She looks good to me."* [20] She was, of course, his undoing.

What we would hope to hear from our candidate for marital bliss is a desire to see some character qualities in the future mate, rather than just a pleasing shape and a nice smell! Does 'loyalty' spring to mind? What about 'faithfulness'? But here's another question: can our single person *force* the prospective partner to be loyal? Is there a guarantee on faithfulness? Definitely not! The 'other party' must be free to choose, and the person's character will be noted as the outcome of those choices. Absolute freedom is an essential context for character

---

20   Judges 14:3 (NASB)

qualities such as loyalty to exist. They cannot be forced upon someone. They are the outcome of choices.

Let's consider an example...

From time to time I leave home to travel off to some far-flung point of the globe. Liberia in West Africa is far enough, but Australia takes the prize for long-haul ministry trips. "Oz" is so far that on the return journey I arrive on the west coast of the United States an hour or so *before* the time I left Sydney, in Australia's southern regions!

When I leave for such a trip I could say to my wife, "Jean, I love you, I trust you and I believe you will be here when I return." Sure enough, when I come back home she is there even though, in the meantime, she has had access to our bank account, our credit card, our home and our car all of which could have been spent or abused in my absence. Jean, in other words, has shown faithfulness and loyalty. I can justifiably say, "You are a faithful wife."

Let's consider another scenario. What if I were to say upon my departure; "Jean, I love you. I trust you. I believe you will be here when I return, but just to make sure I'd like you to step inside this cage. I've provided enough food for three weeks. I'm keeping the key and I'll unlock the cage door upon my return." Would it be logical, as I walked back into the house after my trip, to say, "There, you see, my wife is still here? I *knew* she would be faithful and remain at home. I *knew* she wouldn't squander our finances. She has shown herself to be loyal and true to me and to our marriage."

For loyalty to exist one must have the freedom and ability to be disloyal. To be truly faithful one must have the ability and opportunity to be unfaithful. To be obedient, one must have the freedom to choose the opposite. In other words, one must be *free*. Locked up in her cage Jean could not possibly show loyalty or faithfulness because she had no choice in the matter.

Some years ago I spoke of these things in a conference here in the United States. A dear friend of mine – a man whom I admire – came up to me after I had spoken and said, "Great message Bill and really brave in front of [this crowd]!" Actually, he named the crowd by their doctrinal position and 'this crowd' might have taken an opposing position on some aspects of the freedom of the will. With a smile, I quickly replied, "No, bravery doesn't come into it. If it was pre-destined for me to preach this message before the foundation of the world, then I had no choice, so how could I be called 'brave'?"

Think of it. Can a man be called brave if he is merely acting out a preplanned destiny about which he has no real choice? Or is bravery, along with any other character quality, contingent upon having an alternate choice which stands alongside, offering a convenient and contradictory alternative?

When I was sixteen years old I left my beloved city of Liverpool and went with my parents to Swansea in South Wales. This meant a differ-ent country, a different house, and a different accent and, at times, a different language. I didn't like the idea. Liverpool, after all, was the kind of city that grabs your affections and loyalty by the throat. I had developed the guttural accent of 'The Pool'. I had chosen my football club between the two giants of English soccer whose stadia sat only a mile from each other – Anfield, the home of Liverpool Football Club and Goodison Park, the stadium of Everton. My house was equidis-tant from each, and not very distant, at that!

Although I met some great people in Swansea, my life in that pleasant seaside town proved to be quite lonely. However, in retrospect, some significant and life changing things happened in my brief eighteen month stay in the Land of Song.

First of all, I sang! All my life I had been musical. One could hardly grow up in The Salvation Army without learning to sing in four-part harmony. Reading music and playing several instruments started around the age of seven. But I had never sung 'solo'. In Wales the men are renowned for their singing and I joined in whole-heartedly. So much so that our choir leader eventually said, "Bill, you take the solo in this next section." And what became (and still remains these fifty years later) a main expression of my ministry, was born. Score one for Swansea!

The second bonus of my time in Wales was that it was there God chose to call me into the ministry. Perhaps He was better able to speak to be in my loneliness than He might have been in the loud bustle of Liverpool. Or, more correctly, I was more able to hear Him.

Walking home after a church activity I remember rounding a corner of the steep streets that lead away from the five mile stretch of Swansea Bay and into the Brynmill section of town – and God spoke to me! No booming voice, just a simple certainty. "That's it," I thought. It was as clear. *Crystal!* In an instant I knew I should hand my life over to God and step into the ministry.

I walked the rest of the way home and retired to my bedroom on the third floor. I stood in the bay window from which I could see the entire sweep of the shoreline from the town to The Mumbles, after which came the fabulously wild beaches of the Gower Peninsula. I knelt by my bed, talking to God about what had suddenly entered my mind and heart. After a while I went downstairs to my parents' room to break the news. I knew they would be pleased – delighted, in fact. They had both given their lives to the ministry while still teenagers in the north of Scotland and they had seen their three surviving children grow up strong in the things of God.

I stood at the end of their bed. Mom was almost asleep, while Dad was reading. I stuttered my way through trying to explain what had happened to me out on the street on the way home. My Dad was first to speak. "Well son," he said, "you were dedicated to this before you were born." So, I thought, I am catching up with my destiny!

The idea of having a destiny needs some hard-nosed definition. We are all too ready to fly off into fantasy and fatalism. We see clearly in scripture that God is a destiny-making God. I have come to believe that He does not allow one person to be born to a woman without having, within His heart, a plan and destiny for that life. King David was sure of that when he said, *"All the days ordained for me were written in your book before one of them came to be."* [21] But because we have grown accustomed to good old fatalism, where everything is preplanned by a benevolent god and '*all things work together for the good'*, we assume that every day has been ordained for us and we can't, therefore, go wrong. It's just up to us to live out our destiny however happy or dreadful that might appear to be.

But before surrendering to the fickle finger of fate, let's take a look at what that word 'ordained' really means and what might be meant by God *ordaining* our days and ways.

What we read as 'ordained' comes from the Hebrew term which refers to being shaped or fashioned, to be squeezed into shape as in the hands of a potter. [22] So we can safely assume that God fashioned a life – a destiny – for each of us before we were born. Why would He not do so? Everything He does is done for a wonderful purpose and not least of all the gift of life. But does this mean we are predestined to live that life, as He planned it?

A simple answer to a simple question will settle that one. Have you ever lived an *inordinate* day? Are there days in your life history which you have lived to regret? Would you like a "do over" for some of the wasted days, months, and years? Most definitely! But not if every day was pre-planned and ordained by God and you had no choice in the matter. How could God have planned all that mess, all that sick dysfunctional stupidity? Well, the fact is, He didn't. God ordains that each life should be lived according to His love, His guidance, and His blessing.

---

21   Psalm 139:16
22   Strong's OT:3335 yatsar; to mould into a form;

Peter says that *"God is patient with you, not wanting anyone to per-ish, but everyone to come to repentance."* [23] You'll notice that God's ordained plan for the life of everyone born to woman is stated clearly. He wants 'none to perish but everyone to come to repentance'. You'll also notice that it would be unnecessary for anyone to come to repen-tance had they not first chosen to live contrary to God's will!

So, *'all the days ordained for me'* are upon God's heart. They are the purpose for which I was conceived. Any foolish choice I may have made to live as a rebel, in an inordinate fashion, leads me to the need of another choice. It's called repentance. I am free to choose – one way or the other – and I will be held accountable and fully respon-sible for the outcome of that choice. That is the risk and the reward of freedom, without which it is impossible to properly relate to God, or for that matter, to anyone else.

23   2 Peter 3:9b

5

The Fickle Finger of Fate

FREEDOM OF THE will, the ability to choose, these are the foundations of creativity. Initiative is only present in a life to the degree that that life perceives itself to be free. Initiative is a choice to self-start, to self-motivate, to create something new, to go farther. Ingenuity springs out of freedom of thought and action.

It was not for nothing that America was founded on the words of The United States Declaration of Independence, adopted by the Second Continental Congress on July 4, 1776. The text of the second section of the Declaration of Independence reads: *"We hold these Truths to be self-evident, that all Men are created equal, that they are endowed by their Creator with certain unalienable Rights, that among these are Life, Liberty, and the Pursuit of Happiness."* Freedom was God's idea, for everyone.

Take away that God-given sense of freedom and you will see dull conformity spread over a society like a gray stifling cloud. Just ask those who lived through seventy-five years of Communist totalitarianism in Russia and her surrounding 'allies' and they'll recall the drabness that comes from enforced conformity. On one of my clandestine excursions behind the Iron Curtain I remember gazing at a display which filled the entire window of a large Victorian styled department store, which had obviously seen better days. The window displayed a pyramid about five feet high, made up of gray boxes. I asked a passer-by what they were. She said, "Soap". It was just 'soap', no color, no attractive sales feature, no brand name, no competition. To be fair, they did have a choice – "Take it or leave it!"

In its infancy, the Islamic world was recognized as a hotbed of creativity and innovation. One has only to visit one of my favorite places on Earth, the Andalucían region of southern Spain, to see what used to be the splendor of Islamic art and architecture. As for their music, the complex subtleties of their melodies combined to create a synthesis that has remained in Spain's soul-stirring Flamenco. (Just listen to the *Gipsy Kings!)* Islamic philosophers played host to the nations as - Solomon-like - they displayed their genius to visiting scholars from around Europe.

I paint this picture only to ask one devastating question: What happened!? Where did it all go? Why did it stop?

To a great extent the Islamic empires of old have become desolate dust bowls, failed or failing cultures, which, with all their oil reserves, cannot lift their people out of dreadful poverty. If the Western World ever does shake free of its dependence on Middle-East oil, nations such as Saudi Arabia will be left selling their last natural resource to the United States – 'sand' – to defray our beach erosion after the effects of hurricanes!

My theory is this; any culture which has, at its base, a philosophy of fatalism, will see a deathly decline in creativity and innovativeness.

Perhaps it's unfair to say that Muslims are fatalists. To be theologically correct it would be more accurate to say that they are *Theistic Determinists*. This philosophical position suggests that all events, including man's behavior, are caused by God, and that even freedom itself is not uncaused, but caused by God. To say that God created freedom is one thing, but to suggest that every decision within that so-called freedom is also caused, makes it questionable as to whether we are speaking of actual freedom at all!

I have met very few Arabs who have not shown great kindness, warmth of hospitality and a certain dignity, often in difficult circumstances. But when traveling through the Arab world it doesn't take long to discern the prevailing mind-set, namely that everything is in God's hands – and I mean *everything!* Whether you are speaking about personal health, hygiene, happiness, finding a parking space, trying to get some electrical device to work or waiting for the internet to come back on, a friendly voice nearby will assure you that it will happen soon… but then they add *"in sha Allah"*, "if god wills".

This concept - the belief that everything is being worked out according to the will of God - sounds intensely religious. It is! It's just not necessarily true, at least not 'everything' and not 'all the time'. It may be given a sophisticated philosophical name but it walks like, talks like and sounds like fatalism, which is a submissive mental attitude resulting from acceptance of the doctrine that everything that happens is predetermined and therefore inevitable.

If I build a wall in a village somewhere in the Middle East and it falls down; "In sh' Allah!" If the plumbing, such as it is, fails to work; "In sh' Allah!" If I am fighting a battle against a smaller group of Israelis and they begin to prevail; "In sh' Allah!" If I get a bright idea and think it could make life better for my generation, but I never get round to developing it; well, "In sh' Allah!" The ultimate thought could be, "Maybe I should build my wall back up, or fix my plumbing, but why fight God's will!"

A predetermined world demands no initiative, character, heroism or creativity. I'll go a step farther. Not only does it not demand it, it cannot allow it. All those qualities are evidences of free choice, or else they are in name alone and not in truth.

That which is predetermined must be caused. That which is caused cannot be free. That which is free cannot be pre-destined. That which is pre-destined cannot be punished. Responsibility only rests on the shoulders of the free.

One may have a world where all is predetermined, where every act is predestined, but don't call any or all of those acts 'brave', 'heroic', 'honorable', or even 'disobedient' or 'rebellious'. You can't have it both ways and by the way, the God of The Bible who asks for our obedience and claims to experience pleasure in response to our cooperation and faithfulness, and disappointment at our rebellion, doesn't play "pretend".

This tendency toward fatalism has had some interesting effects on world history and international development. It is interesting that the Islamic fascination with fatalism in southern Europe gave way to the domination of a religious system which was marked by a hierarchical government. Had the people of southern Europe become too acquainted with the idea of a predetermined world? Fatalism, you see, subtly suggests that the lower 'brute' classes were born into their station in society 'by God's will', as were the ruling elite. How can one fight against the Sovereign will of one's Maker?

This attitude of surrendering to one's fate can lead to the acceptance of absolute rule, either by a monarch, a priest, a Pope or a classic dictator. Note the continuation of that spirit as it spread from Spain and Portugal to their colonies in Central and South America and compare it with the different spirit in the Reformation regions of Northern Europe and their subsequent colonization of North America. Having said that, 'surrendering to fate' is an oxymoron. How can one willingly surrender to that which is inevitable and about which there is no choice?

I openly declare my respect and undying affection for my 'second ministry home' in Latin America, but I have to note the fact that the resources of that continent outstrip their neighbors to the north, and yet the level of poverty in South America suggests a lack of a sense of freedom of purpose, initiative, entrepreneurship and social creativity, bred, we might suppose, by generations of autocratic rule from both Church and State. But that rule is only acceptable to a people who feel all things of class and culture are already written and cannot be changed.

How infuriating that Communist revolutionaries would be the ones to fight for the liberty of those oppressed by such fatalism and not the true Church! And yet even Marxism suffers from the curse of the inevitable, even if it is in their preferred direction. They believe in the inevitability of the release and victory of the masses; a noble concept, but does that belief in the inevitable form their downfall?

A fellow pastor and friend of mine once suggested that "You would do better to act more like a dictator here in [South America]." But the attraction to the dictator only shows a tendency toward fatalism, the killer of character. My job is to equip people to become disciples of Jesus whose kingdom does not participate in coercion. *Where the Spirit of the Lord is, there is freedom.* [24]

I was invited to participate in an inter-faith dialogue between a Roman Catholic Priest, a Jewish Rabbi, and an Islamic Imam. I was there to make up 'the rest of the story'. Our lofty subject was 'Religious Diversity and the Epistemic Obligation'. At one point in the discussion we fielded questions from the audience. The Imam, a likable, scholarly and humble man, was asked if he believed that God is a God of love. He answered, "Yes, God is a God of love, but not everyone is loved. If we live by the discipline then we might please Him and He might love us."

In an instant I saw where the all the aggression, anger and frustration in the Muslim world is rooted. If something goes wrong in my life and I believe that everything happens according to God's will and He only loves those who are performing well, then He is obviously displeased with me and I am not yet loved!

---

24   2 Corinthians 3:17

What bondage! What a lie! I was reminded of the scripture, *'We lived in malice and envy, being hated and hating one another. But when the kindness and love of God our Savior appeared, he saved us, not because of righteous things we had done, but because of his mercy.'* [25]

During that forum I stated our assurance that we were loved well before we loved God and that *'God demonstrates his own love for us in this: While we were still sinners, Christ died for us.'* [26]

Let's not blame the Muslims! Fatalism's fickle finger, even when clothed as Theistic Determinism, is also a comfortable refuge for Christians, even those who claim to believe in the freedom of the will and personal responsibility. It's amusing to see how those who believe in freedom of choice often hide behind clichés which sound as if they believe in the predetermination of all things and, just as often, those who believe all things are predestined and cannot be changed, act as if they are very much in charge of their destiny. I like what Steven Hawking said (on a better day), *"I have noticed even people who claim everything is predestined, and that we can do nothing to change it, still look both ways before they cross the road."*

What about those comforting clichés? How about this one, *"we know that all things work together for good..."* [27] Left alone as it is commonly used, this comment seems to suggest that the most appalling situations will somehow work out OK. We can mess up by living a life that is reprobate and wasteful, and it is enough that our praying mothers will hang on to the 'promise' in the Word, that all things will work out to the good.

Have you noticed how frequently we don't complete the entire sentence of scripture when we want it to work out according to our preferences? How about, *"Resist the devil, and he will flee from you."* [28] Sounds nice, doesn't it? Just resist him; he'll flee. However, it's just

---

25   Titus 3:3-5
26   Romans 5:8
27   Romans 8:28 (NKJV)
28   James 4:7

not true, at least not completely true. Ask the sons of Sceva, a Jewish chief priest who tried to resist a demon. *"They would say, 'In the name of Jesus, whom Paul preaches, I command you to come out.' One day the evil spirit answered them, 'Jesus I know, and I know about Paul, but who are you?' Then the man who had the evil spirit jumped on them and overpowered them all. He gave them such a beating that they ran out of the house naked and bleeding.'* [29]

So it might be wise to read 'the rest of the story' and see what James 4:7 really says. It starts, *"Submit yourselves, then, to God. Resist the devil, and he will flee from you."* Do you see the not-so-subtle difference?

It's just like that with our comforting phrase *'All things work together for the good.'* The rest of the story goes like this. *"And we know that all things work together for good to those who love God, to those who are the called according to His purpose."* It is clear, then, that even calamity can befall the people of God, but because of their daily submission to His purposes in their lives, because of their hourly determination to love Him (which is a choice to honor and glorify Him in all things, at all times) everything is placed in His creative, healing and restorative hands and He works it all out to the good.

That 'good', however, is not always what we might have chosen. The Bible nowhere promises that all things will 'work out in the wash' and the believer will get out of the jam and live happily ever after - at least not until he enters Heaven. Throughout history followers of Christ have met with trials and tragedy. Left to themselves they would not have chosen the path of persecution but once they knew Jesus, their choices assumed a higher plain. They were no longer choosing for themselves, but for God's greater glory. What a privilege to have such a facility, to choose God's glory!

Even a brief glance at the history of the Christian Church helps us see how men and women chose to stand strong for Jesus rather than

---

29   Acts 19:13-16

forsake His name. If you divided Church History into pages, page two would announce the following; [30]

Philip:	Crucified, Phrygia, A.D. 54
Matthew:	Beheaded, Ethiopia, A.D. 60
Barnabas:	Burned to death, Cyprus, A.D. 64
Mark:	Dragged to death, Alexandria, A.D. 64
James the Less:	Clubbed to death, Jerusalem, A.D. 66
Paul:	Beheaded, Rome, A.D. 66
Peter:	Crucified upside-down, Rome, A.D. 69
Andrew:	Crucified diagonally (Note my Scottish banner!) Achaia, A.D. 70
Thomas:	Speared to death, Calamina, A.D. 70
Luke:	Hanged, Athens, A.D. 93

My father had three brothers. One was Charles Florence Davidson. Only the Victorians could explain where the 'Florence' part came from! Before the Second World War, Uncle Charlie went to Japan as a missionary. In those days that great nation was centuries 'older' than it is today!

The war came and Japan joined the actual 'Axis of Evil'. As the Allies lost ground, Charlie's wife Bodil and their daughter, my cousin Renee, escaped, leaving husband and father behind to continue his ministry. It wasn't long before he was interned in a Prisoner of War Camp. Because of his fluent Japanese, he was appointed the Camp Chaplain. Among his duties he was to taste the 'food' each morning and assure the camp commandant that all was well. He soon learned that to refuse the insect-ridden slop was to deny the men any food at all, so he chose to determine the food 'acceptable'. He didn't know it, but some of those insects are full of protein!

At the war's end, the Japanese guards abandoned the camp to be liberated by the invading Allies. One by one the prisoners returned to their homes and their families. Uncle Charlie remained until the last

---

30 Taken from Church Tradition

man was released and repatriated. Only then did he begin his long journey home to Aberdeen in the North East of Scotland. He arrived ten days after his beloved wife Bodil had succumbed to cancer.

Before long, my Uncle returned to Japan. Like St. Patrick - another Scot from generations before who was enslaved by the Irish - after his release Charlie returned to the land of his oppressors. It was also the land and the people he loved.

He walked among the ruins of what had been the Tokyo headquarters of his denomination. Out of the ruins walked a man, looking not much better than a ragged beggar. It was one of the great leaders of the Church in Japan. One would hope that the two of them would have embraced, but no, this was Japan! As their tear stained eyes met, the old saint said, "We knew you would return, David-san."

Uncle Charlie received the M.B.E. [31] for his services to the Empire but he would be the last to make mention of such things. He simply lived out the consequences of his choices. He could have made life easier for himself. With his extensive knowledge of Japanese culture, and the complexities of the language, he could have ingratiated himself with the commandant and yet a testimony of his treatment came weeks later when, safe and surrounded by my family in our home in England, my mother would bring him breakfast in bed. Each morning, she told us years later, he would cower to the corner of his bed, arms raised over his head to ward off the worst of being kicked awake – daily.

Here is your question: Did Charles Davidson show bravery? How about Luke, Matthew, Patrick? What about that youngster Mark, who was probably the boy who fled the Garden of Gethsemane [32] and no more than about forty years old when he met his death. What of the thousands who did not return home after the Second World War? Were they truly brave? Was it a choice, or were they simply living out a predetermined path which was unavoidable?

---

31 The Most Excellent Order of the British Empire; an order of chivalry established on 4 June 1917 by King George V of the United Kingdom

32 Mark 14:51

More seriously still, what of those who gave in to torture, who sided with the enemy, who betrayed their fellow prisoners, who renounced Christ at the first sight of the lions and bears of the Roman Coliseum? Did they show cowardice, or did God write their miserable script somewhere in the heavenlies, before it all happened by the fore-or-daining finger of fate?

6

But Isn't God Sovereign?

TO SOME, THE idea of humans having a free choice toward their destiny is nothing less than an affront to the Sovereignty of God. To my way of thinking, anything less would be an affront to His justice.

One well known radio Bible teacher reasoned that if a man has the ability of self-determination, it would be a waste of time and effort to pray for that man's salvation. He reasoned, "What could God do in order to save him?" The truth is to the contrary. If a man's salvation is predetermined by God, leaving the individual no choice, then *that* would seem to make any prayer on his behalf to be truly redundant.

The radio teacher's argument implied that man's salvation is pre-determined by God, so whether he likes it or not, he will be saved – or otherwise. It also implied that those who believe in the freedom of the will suggest that man, by the action of that will, can bring about his own salvation, which he cannot. It further implied that a God who lovingly woos His lost loved-ones, without predetermining their response, is somehow impotent. Yet that wooing and the absence of coercion is the clear testimony of Scripture.

One could add, what would be the use of praying for someone whose eternity *is* already predetermined. In fact, in a predetermined world what is the use of requests in prayer, for anything?

John McArthur writes, "[God] *chose them [those being saved] solely because it pleased Him to do so. God declare the end from the beginning, saying, 'My purpose will be established, and I will accomplish all My good pleasure.'* [33] *He is not subject to others' decisions. His purposes for choosing some and rejecting others are hidden in the secret counsels of His own will."* [34]

This is a compelling argument. No-one can dispute God's right to do whatever He pleases, nor could we question His right to exact punishment on the wicked, which, whether we like it or not, could be any or all of us. The question is, would He? Is that consistent with His character and values? Is He, in that 'secret counsel of His own will' so arbitrary as to condemn some and redeem others simply on the basis of His right to do so?

A friend of mine told the story of a preacher who stated to him that God's sovereign choice to save some, was as if He walked into the Death Row of a penitentiary, full of men deserving to die, and said: "You, you, and you… redeemed. Go free!" The preacher added "What could we say to a God like that?" By all means this would be a display of His great mercy, but only partially. What we *could* say to that God is obvious: "What about the rest? Did you not love them also?"

My friend's response was, "You are saying that salvation is all of God's choosing. But if that is so, why does He save so few? And I – a one-lunged preacher - am seeking to save all I can. That, sir, means your God loves sinners less than I do."

I would like you to consider that to be a sovereign does not mean to control everything, all the time. That's not a sovereign, that's a dictator!

---

33 Isaiah 46:10
34 *Adapted from John MacArthur's book 'Ashamed of the Gospel' published by Crossway Books.*

Being sovereign can just as easily mean that God may do what He desires to do; what He sovreignly chooses to do. As the Psalmist says, *"Our God is in heaven; He does whatever pleases him."* [35] As sovereign He may choose to predetermine all things, and although it would seem arbitrary and lacking in pure justice, He may choose which sinners to pardon and which to condemn. On the other hand He may choose to create a species which is free to choose Him, free to love Him, free to value Him over all else, and therefore, equally free to ignore and disregard Him, even though He warns of the dire consequences of such behavior. Does this make Him less sovereign?

Not one act of God will be open to question in the courts of final things but Satan will hope for any morsel of evidence to bring a charge against God, claiming He has been either overly merciful or inordinately legal.

The dilemma in the Atonement is that it must satisfy both tenets of God's throne; justice and mercy. Justice is the foundation of God's government. Mercy is the desire and the outcome of God's heart. The Psalmist writes, *"Righteousness and justice are the foundation of your throne."* [36] God's mercy is emblazoned everywhere in His word, *"How can I give you up, Ephraim? How can I hand you over, Israel? How can I treat you like Admah? How can I make you like Zeboiim? My heart is changed within me; all my compassion is aroused. I will not carry out my fierce anger, nor will I turn and devastate Ephraim. For I am God, and not man – the Holy One among you. I will not come in wrath."* [37]

So I propose to you the idea that our Sovereign God does what He pleases and always what is best. By all means, from time to time, He will cause certain things to take place by His sovereign interjection. If He did not do so, then the unfolding of history would slip from His plans and purposes, something He would never allow to happen as it would prove Him to be less than trustworthy.

35   Psalm 115:3
36   Psalm 89:14
37   Hosea 11:8,9

Yet we must ask the question, would God hold people responsible for these divine interjections He Himself makes; things which He Himself has caused? Would a God of justice cause someone's rebellion and then, on that great Day of Judgment, condemn that same person for his actions even though the man in question had no part in initiating them? If I were Satan, I'd already be rising to my feet to cry "Objection!" And wouldn't the Accuser of the Brethren delight in doing that? [38]

To illustrate this interjection of God's sovereign strategy, let's take a look at some of those moments in history when He has caused things to happen - some of the momentary acts that turned the tide of epic events - some points in the progression of things which could not be left to the vacillations of human choice.

A classic example of this was when God hardened the heart of Pharaoh against the idea of allowing Israel to go free. Exodus chapter ten states, *"Then the LORD said to Moses, 'Go to Pharaoh, for I have hardened his heart and the hearts of his officials so that I may perform these miraculous signs of mine among them that you may tell your children and grandchildren how I dealt harshly with the Egyptians and how I performed my signs among them, and that you may know that I am the Lord."* [39]

It's as clear as a bell! God hardened Pharaoh's heart and caused him to choose in a certain direction. In the original language it says God bound up, restrained, or conquered the heart of Pharaoh. But here is our question: Do you think Pharaoh will be held responsible for that moment's decision on the Day of Judgment?

The Bible states clearly, *"And I saw the dead, great and small, standing before the throne, and books were opened. Another book was opened, which is the book of life. The dead were judged according to what they had done as recorded in the books. The sea gave up*

---

38   Revelation 12:10
39   Exodus 10:1,2

the dead that were in it, and death and Hades gave up the dead that were in them, and each person was judged according to what he had done." [40] Notice, twice the Bible states that people will be judged for what they have done, but at no point does it suggest that man will be judged for what God has done, even if He used a man through which to do it.

The same principle applies in the action of the gifts of the Holy Spirit. No person will be judged as being extra special because they prophesied or healed the sick or gained some word of knowledge, even though in our generation we all but deify such ministers. These things were the actions of God wrought through a human vessel, a clay pot. [41] The person in question might be noted for being available to God's Spirit in that moment and should be encouraged for being a willing vessel, but no more than that. God will not give glory or judgment for things He Himself has done. That would not be just, not even logical, and - despite what some would suggest – God is logical. He invented it.

So, for what will Pharaoh be judged if not for that moment when God made sure his heart remained hard? I've already given away the answer by using the term 'remained'. On at least two other occasions Pharaoh is described as hardening his heart against God and Israel. [42] God was not about to allow any momentary softening of this ruthless ruler to stand in the way of the judgment he was about to inflict on Egypt. God was setting things up for nothing less than The Exile of His people Israel, and the foibles of a Pharaoh were not going to interrupt His schedule at such a crucial time in history. It might also be noted that God would be fully aware of several other skeletons in Pharaoh's closet, so what He did in causing this momentary hardening of the heart was hardly out of character in the case of Egypt's king.

Another example of God sovreignly interjecting His purposes into the history of mankind came at another great moment which could not

---

40   Revelation 20:12,13
41   2 Corinthians 4:7
42   Exodus 8:15 & 32

be left to the choices of a generation. The Incarnation was about to take place. Can you think of anything more significant? Every detail must be in place and must happen in God's consecutive order; at just the right time. [43]

One of these details, an essential which could not be left to the vagaries of human choice, was the appearance of John the Baptist, *"the voice of one crying in the wilderness: 'Prepare the way of the Lord; Make straight in the desert, a highway for our God.'"* [44] That statement alone had been waiting about six hundred years to be fulfilled, so nothing could be left to chance for its revelation.

John the Baptist was the last of the Old Testament prophets who 'snuck' into the New Testament by a hair's breadth – and by all accounts he had plenty of hair to spare. Every prophet before John had, in some way or another, pointed toward the coming of the Messiah, some more than others. But John, he was the one appointed to point – literally – across a few feet of the Jordan River and exclaim, *"Look, the Lamb of God, who takes away the sin of the world!"* [45] Now it's one thing to point, figuratively, toward the coming Messiah, as did Isaiah and others, but it is entirely another thing to point with your finger! "Him...that one...on the far bank...to the left of that bush..."

So how did God's sovereignty show up in John's life? God had called many other prophets before, with varying levels of success. Some had superlative records while others, well, they did OK. You might recall how one was eaten by a lion on the way home from his first mission – a successful but somewhat protracted ministry! No such mishap could be allowed when it came to the very last Old Testament prophet.

For starters, John was baptized in the Holy Spirit while still in the womb! Now, I've heard some people proclaim, "I was born a Baptist and will be buried a Baptist." This was a little more dramatic that that. John was born a Pentecostal!

43   Romans 5:6
44   Isaiah 40:3 & Matthew 3:3
45   John 1:29,30

The scriptures tell us that Mary, the mother of Jesus, while still carrying her firstborn, went to visit her cousin Elizabeth, in whose womb was the prophet John. Even as Mary walked toward her, *"Elizabeth heard Mary's greeting, the baby leaped in her womb, and Elizabeth was filled with the Holy Spirit."* [46] I fully believe Elizabeth's experience was an outcome of what was already happening to the child within her. God, in His sovereignty, was meeting with the divinely appointed child. The Angel of The Lord spoke to John's father, promising, *"he will be filled with the Holy Spirit even from birth."* [47]

From that moment on, John was a person set apart for his appointed task. He was born for a specific time in human history and for a specific purpose. No idling away the days of his childhood. Not for him the games of adolescence. He became a man of the desert. He was literally set aside for God's purposes.

He lived His life under the sovereign management of God. His every step was under God's causation. Nothing else was permissible at such a moment in history. Look at how he is described:

"In those days John the Baptist came, preaching in the Desert of Judea and saying, 'Repent, for the kingdom of heaven is near.' This is he who was spoken of through the prophet Isaiah: A voice of one calling in the desert, Prepare the way for the Lord, make straight paths for him. John's clothes were made of camel's hair and he had a leather belt around his waist. His food was locusts and wild honey. People went out to him from Jerusalem and all Judea and the whole region of the Jordan. Confessing their sins, they were baptized by him in the Jordan River.' [48]

Jesus spoke of Him this way: *"What did you go out into the desert to see? A reed swayed by the wind? If not, what did you go out to see? A man dressed in fine clothes? No, those who wear fine clothes are in kings' palaces. Then what did you go out to see? A prophet? Yes,*

---

46 Luke 1:41,42
47 Luke 1:15
48 Matthew 3:1-6

I tell you, and more than a prophet. This is the one about whom it is written: 'I will send my messenger ahead of you, who will prepare your way before you.'" [49]

John's singleness of purpose, the fire in his eyes, the passion of his message, was heaven-sent. None of this came by way of man's teaching. No earthly school gave him such zeal. He was like a flame in the darkness, like the dawn after a four hundred year silent night.

The last words of the Old Testament rang out into that long silence, *"See, I will send you the prophet Elijah before that great and dreadful day of the Lord comes."* [50] Then, as John's father stood in the presence of God at the right side of the altar of incense [51] an angel spoke those very same words back to him. He spoke of the son in Elizabeth's womb, *"And he will go on before the Lord, in the spirit and power of Elijah, to turn the hearts of the fathers to their children and the disobedient to the wisdom of the righteous — to make ready a people prepared for the Lord."*

Here is a man, from birth immersed in the sovereign causation of God. Surely he was predestined to walk through life, from his first step to his last, fulfilling God's purposes? Where did personal choice come in? God is sovereign. John was chosen. But wait! A strange episode happened just hours before John was to meet his death by the executioner's sword. Languishing in prison, this prophet who had never uttered a word of compromise or doubt, never took an uncertain step, this man who was given the inestimable privilege of being the actual one to proclaim *"Behold, the Lamb"*; he asked a few of his disciples to skip across town with a message for Jesus. And what did he ask? Here are his words: *"Are you the one who was to come, or should we expect someone else?"* [52]

It is astonishing that such words should come out of the same mouth

---

49   Matthew 11:7-10
50   Malachi 4:5
51   Luke 1:11-17
52   Matthew 11:3

that had been, from the first day of his ministry, a solid rock of certainty. There can be only one explanation. The sovereignty of God had lifted off. Just like the rest of us John had to choose what he personally believed about Jesus. Let's face it, no-one will be asked any more than this, *"But what about you?"* Jesus will ask. *"Who do you say I am?"* [53] And in this moment, sitting alone in a condemned cell, John had to work out the answer for himself.

No one will enter the kingdom because God caused him to believe. Coercion has no place in a love relationship. It's a choice, and a choice John had to make apart from the sovereign causation his life had known since the womb.

It's interesting to note Jesus' reply, *"Go back and report to John what you hear and see: The blind receive sight, the lame walk, those who have leprosy are cured, the deaf hear, the dead are raised, and the good news is preached to the poor. Blessed is the man who does not fall away on account of me."* [54] In other words, "Make up your mind. It's time to decide." There was no clear 'Yes', or 'No'. It was time for John to get his head together on these matters because very soon he was to lose it.[55]

Consider Jesus' description of John, *"I tell you the truth: Among those born of women there has not risen anyone greater than John the Baptist; yet he who is least in the kingdom of heaven is greater than he."* [56] Many reasons may have been in the Lord's heart when He uttered those words, but I have often wondered whether He was referring to the fact that John's entire life had not been of his own choosing, save the last few hours, and for these few hours alone he would be held responsible. The years before had been by God's sovereignty, by God's causation. John, the greatest prophet of all time, made it into the kingdom of God in his last few hours, by the skin of his teeth.

---

53   Matthew 16:15
54   Matthew 11:4-6
55   Matthew 14:9,10
56   Matthew 11:11

7

Whatever Happened to Stoning?

WE OFTEN LOOK at the testimony of men and women of God and see how God sovreignly met with them, assuming this was because they had a specific role to play in God's plans, inferring that they had little or no choice in the matter. Such a one is Saul of Tarsus, later to be known by his Roman name, Paul. It seems obvious that God sovreignly intervened in his life by meeting him on the road to Damascus in such a dramatic way. Let Paul describe it himself and you'll catch this no-so-subtle intrusion of God's sovereignty:

"About noon, O king, as I was on the road, I saw a light from heaven, brighter than the sun, blazing around me and my companions. We all fell to the ground, and I heard a voice saying to me in Aramaic, 'Saul, Saul, why do you persecute me? It is hard for you to kick against the goads.' Then I asked, 'Who are you, Lord?' 'I am Jesus, whom you are persecuting,'" [57]

May we conclude that Saul was predestined to become the great Apostle Paul? Or did he have a choice in the matter? Notice that after such a supernatural manifestation it seems Paul was still free to choose his destiny. True, God sovreignly intervened in Paul's life, but not upon his personal responsibility to choose or refuse a relationship with the Father through Jesus Christ. He continued his narration

---

57   Acts 26:12-15

of the story in this way: *"So then, King Agrippa, I was not disobedient to the vision from heaven,"* [58] inferring that he fully realized he was free to be so. God, in His sovereignty, had interrupted Paul's journey, but notice that He chose not to cross the line of Paul's will, because there, in the place of his choices, he would be held responsible and accountable for his entire life on that Great Day.

It is fascinating to notice these 'moments in history' where God does not allow the free choice of humankind to steer events haphazardly. The acting out of the Atonement – my favorite subject of all time – is one such historical event.

The very purpose for which God became incarnate [59] was about to be fulfilled and one of the prerequisites for this epic event was that it must be a gift of God and not enacted by the hand of man. How, we may ask, could the act of atonement be meted out by the violent hand of sinful humanity? Jesus said, *"I lay down my life — only to take it up again. No one takes it from me, but I lay it down of my own accord."* [60] Salvation truly is a free gift of God and could not be accomplished by the hand of the recipient.

Having established that, we now ask the question: What was the lawful punishment for the charges against Jesus? The Jewish authorities made that clear, *"the high priest tore his clothes and said, 'He [Jesus] has spoken blasphemy! Why do we need any more witnesses? Look, now you have heard the blasphemy. What do you think?'"* [61]

If this Jesus was merely a man who claimed to be God, then it was blasphemy, clearly! So what must the judgment be? The law allowed that the blasphemer must be taken *'outside the camp'* and publicly stoned.[62] But here lies a dilemma. Not only must the atonement include the death of the spotless lamb, but it must be a death which

---

58   Acts 26:19
59   Embodied in flesh; given a bodily form
60   John 10:17,18
61   Matthew 26:65,66
62   Leviticus 24:13-23

allows enough time for Christ to take upon Himself - actively, willingly and *consciously* – the sins of mankind, and this cannot be at the hands of the guilty! Therefore stoning is unacceptable. The first or second stone hurled at the head of Jesus would render Him unconscious. Where then would stand the act of atonement?

It is at this moment God stepped in, sovreignly, with divine causation, to see another path created. It was acted out as Jesus stood before Pontius Pilate. The Roman governor found no fault in this man, so he turned to the crowd and said, *"I will punish him and then release him."* [63] But the crowd would have nothing of that, so for the first and last time in history, a crowd of Jewish men shouted against a blasphemer, *"Crucify him! Crucify him!"*

Whatever happened to stoning? Had they, en masse, suffered a case of doctrinal amnesia? Did they think stoning had become too barbaric? Had they begun to ignore the law? Obviously not. Within a few short weeks the same people thought nothing of condemning Stephen to death - the first Christian martyr - stoned for the same crime, blasphemy.

For the atonement to be fulfilled the Lamb of God could not be allowed to die a violent death at the hand of sinful man. Not for Him a crushing fall under a pile of rocks thrown by vengeful sinners. And amazingly, even crucifixion did not cause His demise! Mankind added nothing toward it save their terrible rebellion.

So, how and why did Jesus die? It's an important question. Important to everyone, not least those millions of Jews murdered as 'Christ killers' when Fascist dictators made it their doctrine of convenience. But neither Judaism nor the might of Rome had the slightest ability to kill the Christ. God did not allow it. He intervened, sovreignly altering the minds and actions of a legalistic and self righteous crowd.

The act of atonement was not just a case of arranging for Jesus to be killed as a sacrificial lamb. It was a conscious choice, a process

---

63   Luke 23:16

which would take a period of time. This was no 'eye for an eye' act of heroism. It started long before Jesus said, *"Father, into your hands I commit my spirit"* and then He *'breathed his last.'* [64]

Hours before, in the garden of Gethsemane, Jesus spent the night in prayer. Earlier that night he had shared the Passover Supper with His disciples during which He had taken one of the ceremonial cups of the Pesach [65] and declared, *"This cup is the new covenant in my blood, which is poured out for you."* [66] Later, in the garden, hours before the first scourge was lashed to his back, [67] the blood of the atonement began to flow.

It is interesting that Luke, the physician, was the only gospel writer to record the fact that Jesus, *"being in anguish, he prayed more earnestly, and his sweat was like drops of blood falling to the ground."* [68] This evidence of hematidrosa was a testimony to the extreme stress experienced by the holy, spotless Lamb of God as He began to take into His pure and righteous being the filthy residue of the world's sin. This was the beginning of His death, not at the hands of humanity, but by the grace outpoured by a redeeming God.

Further testimony that Jesus died of His own choice and not by scourging, or even by crucifixion, came at the very end. The Roman soldiers had a way of ensuring the ultimate death of their crucified victims, who out of some profound will to survive would prolong their lives through incredible effort. Time and again they would press down against the nails in their feet, in order to stretch their pain-wracked body to its full height in order to fill their lungs with another desperate breath of air. Then, relaxing again (if one could call it relaxation) they would once more take the weight of their body on their impaled arms. As long as the victim could repeat this agonizing process determined how long they could survive. Some would live on for days.

---

64   Luke 23:46
65   The Jewish term for Passover
66   Luke 22:20
67   John 19:1
68   Luke 22:43,44

The soldiers, hearing that the Jewish authorities had requested that the bodies not be left hanging throughout the Sabbath,[69] went about their business with usual thoroughness. Their efficient strategy was to break the legs of each victim, thus ensuring his inability to raise himself up to take that next vital breath. Death quickly followed by suffocation. Crucifixion was just the show case for the struggle for life, the 'display board', the public stage for the epic drama.

However, when they came to Jesus, they found Him already dead.[70] This was unusual. He was a strong young man in his early thirties. A carpenter by trade, He had spent the last several years walking the open roads. This was no scholarly weakling. To make sure of His death, John's gospel states, *"they did not break his legs. Instead, one of the soldiers pierced Jesus' side with a spear, bringing a sudden flow of blood and water. The man who saw it has given testimony, saying "and his testimony is true. He knows that he tells the truth, and he testifies so that you also may believe."'*[71]

It seems that John was moved by the Holy Spirit to add this testimony at the end of the story. Was He simply testifying to the fact of Christ's death – a report which was disputed by the Jewish authorities after His resurrection – or did the Spirit of God inspire those words for a greater reason? This flow of blood and water was yet another medical testimony to the cause of Christ's death. The Roman soldier drove his spear up through the pericardium, which, as its name suggests, surrounds the heart. The issue was not actual blood and water. Blood was there, certainly, but the 'water' John saw was a bile-like liquid which had gathered around the heart, inside the pericardial sac. These days we would call it *pericardial effusion* and there can be several causes. I believe the release of sickness, disease and even sin itself (or at least its consequences) into the physical body of Our Savior was more than adequate cause.

Christ did not die from crucifixion, at the hands of sinful humanity. He died of His own choosing; taking whatever time He needed to

---

69 John 19:31
70 John 19:32
71 John 19:33-35

accomplish the task at hand. He died - literally – of a ruptured broken heart. And God sovreignly managed every moment of risk, every minute when the crowd's ugly rage could have taken over, until His will was performed. God is Sovereign, and as such can be trusted to accomplish His purposes in amongst the chaos of human life.

At any time during those crucial hours leading up to the crucifixion, in the garden, during the trials and the beatings and upon the cross itself, Jesus could have died at the hands of man. No wonder He said, *"My Father, if it is possible, may this cup be taken from me,"* [72] not out of fear of death – His sacrificial death was why He had come to Earth - but so that the will of the Father might prevail. By His sovereign intervention God kept murder at bay, even the law of capital punishment itself was set aside, sovreignly, so that the Atonement might be fulfilled, to the last full measure.

God need not micromanage every breath of each human being or every flap of the butterfly's wings in order to keep things in line with His ultimate plans and purposes. He is bigger than that. He is God. He is Sovereign.

---

72   Matthew 26:39

8

Does God Make Choices?

THE IDEA THAT God might exercise an act of will, from the context of His love, is to some people quite disconcerting. It is easier and more secure for them to consider God as an unchanging immutable Being whose consistency lies in the fact that His every future action is already prescribed. His immutability [73] and eternity are qualities they would translate as being *'the same yesterday, today and forever.* [74] But must this 'sameness' mean boring inaction? Could it not just as easily mean a consistent, interactive and dependable faithfulness?

Some people believe that for God to be 'eternal' He must be beyond or somehow outside the passage of time. They think of Him in a time-less and therefore unchanging zone, apart from and uninvolved in the vicissitudes of the created order.

This view, however, comes from man's perspective, not God's. Time, to mankind, is a measurement of life segmented by the movement of planets in relation to one another. The days, weeks, months and seasons are brought about by the inter-reaction of planets and stars. Earthlings can hope they might exist long enough for our planet to circumnavigate our Sun eighty or ninety times. Yet time exists beyond our solar system and even beyond our universe, so

---

73   Immutable = unchanging through time; unalterable; ageless:
74   Hebrews 13:8

it cannot adequately be measured as we would record the days of our lives.

This extraterrestrial definition of time must simply be seen as 'a sequence of events'. That's what time is: *a sequence of events*. It's ludicrous for us to imagine that the angels count their existence by how many times Earth rotates around the sun! They live in a different neighborhood, only visiting ours – from time to time.

Does God dwell within such a sequence? Seemingly, He does. There was a time before He created the universe; a time when *"He spoke, and it was,"* [75] and a time when He reviewed His recent actions and declared them to be *'good'.'* [76] Does that seem to suggest a sequence?

Does the testimony of Scripture acknowledge that God has a memory? If so, is that memory only of your past or of His also? God is recorded as having said, *"Whenever I bring clouds over the earth and the rainbow appears in the clouds, I will remember my covenant between me and you and all living creatures of every kind,"* [77] and, *"This is what the Sovereign Lord says: I will deal with you as you deserve, because you have despised my oath by breaking the covenant. Yet I will remember the covenant I made with you in the days of your youth, and I will establish an everlasting covenant with you."* [78] In this way God is shown to be interactive with His creation.

Throughout the Hebrew scriptures God is revealed as enjoying a dynamic and responsive relationship with His creation in a give-and-take fashion. The Bible shows that He genuinely interacts with humanity by the exercise of His will. As a result, God's life exhibits transition, development and variation.

Nowhere is such a dynamic and interactive relationship more clearly shown than early in the testimony of Scripture when the record says:

---

75   Psalm 33:6-9
76   Genesis 1:25
77   Genesis 9:14,15
78   Ezekiel 16:59-61

"The Lord was sorry that He had made man on the Earth and He was grieved in His heart." [79]

Now, make up your mind. Was God sorry as a direct response to something He had seen and experienced, or was He just pretending to be sorry to make us think of Him as being more personally involved with us than He actually is?

Jonah is recorded as being frustrated with a trait in God's character in that he fully expected that God might exercise an alternate choice to one already made. He feared that God might relent of His first course of action and choose another strategy in response to the repentance of the Ninevites. *"I knew that You are a gracious and compassionate God,"* he complained, *"slow to anger and abounding in love, a God who relents from sending calamity."* [80]

His frustration was justified! After a warning that they would be destroyed in forty days, the people of Nineveh fasted and prayed and repented, and God *"had compassion and did not bring upon them the destruction He had threatened."* [81]

This God, who obviously exercises His free choice by contemplating alternate actions to bring about His will, selecting His response in dynamic interaction with mankind's obedience or rebellion, is entirely consistent with the testimony of Scripture, and mirrored in our hopes and expectations of Him, if not always in our theology.

It is interesting to note that those who believe God's course is already set in eternal stone still believe in intercessory prayer! Moses related to God in this way when He asked God to *"turn from Your fierce anger"* and to *"relent and do not bring disaster on Your people."* [82] He had reason to be concerned! God had already promised to utterly

---

79 Genesis 6:6
80 Jonah 4:2
81 Jonah 3:10
82 Exodus 32:12

destroy Israel and begin a new nation under Moses. [83] Whereas most of us would have quite happily accepted God's choice to start an entirely new brand of humanity from our seed (a fairly conspicuous place in anyone's family tree), Moses chose a more humble route. He interceded with God, asking Him to change His strategy.

Moses' intercession worked. Exodus records that *"the Lord relented (The New American Standard Bible says God 'changed His mind') and did not bring on His people the disaster He had threatened."* [84]

Again, let's ask the hard questions. Did God really relent of something He had promised to do, or was He just pretending to threaten Israel, enacting some sort of divinely mysterious trickery? "Nudge, nudge, wink, wink…I wouldn't really have destroyed them, but they weren't to know, were they? And anyway, it worked!"

Many commentators have difficulties with the idea of God changing His plans in relational response to His creation. R. Alan Cole says that this text is evidence of an anthropomorphism - or more accurately an anthropopathism, [85] a description of God's actions in purely human terms. *'It does not mean that God changed His mind;" says Cole, "still less that He regretted something that He had intended to do. It means …that He now embarked on a different course from that already suggested as a possibility.'* [86]

If Cole is correct, then God made the suggestion of the first course of action with no intention of making it available, so what Cole calls a *'possibility'* was nothing of the sort. And notice that Cole insists that for God to change His course would entail Him suffering regret over His first choice of action. *("Whoops! Sorry, I got that wrong.")* Not at bit! Both courses of action were entirely righteous and justified. The change came to the delight of God, not to His regret!

---

83 Exodus 32:10
84 Exodus 32:12
85 Anthropopathism = ascription of human passions to a being or beings not human, esp. to a deity.
86 R. Alan Cole, Exodus: An Introduction and Commentary Intervarsity Press, 1973

Stephen Charnock thinks in similar lines. He claims that God does not "turn" from a given action, but that man turns in response to God. The circumstances change, not because God changes, but because of man's response. [87] However, the text does not support this theory. It is plain that God exercised His will by changing His action in response to the intercession of Moses, and not because of any repentance in the hearts of the people. In fact when Moses returned to the Israelites after God's changed position, they were still deeply committed to idolatry. [88]

Although it appears to be the clear testimony of Scripture, the idea of a God who responds by the action of His free will, within a sequence of time, or a God who even waits to gauge the responses of man before choosing His own response, will be challenged by those who stress God's immutability, His 'unchangeableness'. By this, some mean that God cannot and will not change in any way, whatsoever. They argue that any change suffered by a perfect God would render Him less than perfect. But surely if a perfect being changes himself, He will do it...perfectly!

The Bible makes it clear that the immutability of God is focused on His faithfulness and trustworthiness as a relational and personal Being. But some have taken His immutability in quite another direction and turned it into immobility and inertia.

The idea of a God who is changeless - in the sense that the perfect, if changed, becomes less than perfection - is found in the thinking of Plato. He says that change is impossible in God since if he changes at all he can only change for the worse. [89] Plato's glass, it would seem, was always half empty!

Plato continues to consider the immutability factor of God's character as inferring changelessness even in His emotions. *"God is most blest*

---

87   Charnock, Existence & Attributes of God
88   Exodus 32:15-29
89   Plato Republic 381- Dialogues of Plato – Random House 1937

and happy a being, experiencing no joy or sorrow." [90] If that is Plato's definition of happiness, one wonders what sort of marriage the poor man 'enjoyed', and one would be reticent to sing, "Happy Birthday, dear Plato!"

Greek philosophy and its unbiblical concepts plainly did not end at the advent of Christianity. Some of the Early Church Fathers were influenced by such thinking. The bridge that began with Plato was crossed by Aristotle, the Stoics, and Philo, and sadly it was extended by such notable Christian theologians as Ignatius and Justin Martyr.

Ignatius, who died in 107 A.D., described God as timeless, invisible and impassable, [91] and yet at the same time he allowed for the suffering of Jesus. But doesn't suffering involve a process of change? So he has already disproved his concept of Christ being impassable. In fact, the Incarnation itself is a process of change. Stranger still, Ignatius does not seem to allow for suffering in the Person of God, The Father, while confessing it in the Person of the Son.[92] Surely this brings an unacceptable dichotomy into the Godhead. And even if one allows such a separation, are we to suppose that the Father felt no pain for His righteous, holy Son?

Justin Martyr was attracted to Greek concepts of God, to the extent of saying that He is unchangeable, incomprehensible, and impassable. Whereas he rejected the Epicurean concept that the gods do not concern themselves with human affairs, he still struggles to reconcile Greek philosophy with biblical revelation, declaring that although there are no passions in God (how could an unchanging Being experience passion?) He still cares for us. After all, *'He is not a stone.'* [93] Make up your mind, Justin!

Origen was an early Christian scholar and theologian, living at the

---

90   Plato Laws 900-907
91   Ignatius Epistle to Polycarp 3:2 & Epistle to Ephesians 7
92   Scottish Journal of Theology 1968 The Pagan Dogma of The Absolute Unchangeableness of God
93   Justin Martyr First Apology - 28

turn of the first century, and one of the most distinguished writers of the early Christian Church. No one can doubt his genius, and yet he seemed confused when describing God's responses to man. In some early homilies he correctly declared God's position in rejoicing at human conversion and His sorrow over human sin. He went on to state that God the Father experiences the emotions of suffering, pity and love. In this it seems he was determined to defend the idea of God's ability to have a genuine relationship with His created order. Yet, when defining God's immutability and impassability, he states that God experiences uninterrupted happiness, and that all of the scriptures with reference to the passions of God are anthropomorphisms, used because of human weakness, and not to be taken literally. [94]

It is not uncommon for philosophers to have one set of ideas for man and yet another and contradictory set of principles in place when attempting to describe God. The easy way out is to call this a 'mystery', which most of the time means they just haven't been able to think it through to their own satisfaction, or that common sense might lead them to some conclusions with which they would rather not grapple. I witnessed the same response in my Bible College days when a teacher was faced with a student's question for which he (or she) had no apparent answer!

In this position Origen reflected that of Philo, [95] who held that the idea of God repenting of a position, or in any way changing in reaction to circumstances, was not to be taken literally. He also thought that such references were anthropomorphisms for the *"duller folk"* who would not understand the true nature of God! That's a good cop-out. Next we'll be seeing a separation of a superior priesthood from those dull lay people! Oh, wait a minute, that 'is' what happened!

Mixed in with the foundations of Christian thinking, and back into the

---

94   Origen De Principles 2.4.4. Contra Celcus 4:37, 72; 6.53
95   Philo Judaeus lived in Alexandria, Egypt, from 20 B.C. to 40 A.D. He was a Jew in religion but a Greek in philosophy, and did much to promote this fusion of thought. The selection below describes the pre-Christian ascetics of Egypt. It is important because it shows that asceticism was common in the deserts of Egypt even before the Christian monks and thus by no means peculiarly Christian.

concepts of Greek philosophy, which so often invaded the Church's earliest apologists, many scholars sought to explain away what the scriptures simply and clearly state, that God is a personal being, complete with desires, responses and emotions, in other words, dynamic and personal.

The revelation of God in the testimony of Scripture in no way marries with the inert god of Greek philosophy or of some theological concepts. The God of the Bible is personal, dynamic and responsive to His creation. In fact He possesses all the attributes of personality He has so graciously bestowed upon mankind.

There are three attributes without which personality cannot exist: a mind, a will & emotions. Without these three, a meaningful relationship is impossible.

The mind is the residence of the ability to think, reason, remember, imagine and create. The Bible is replete with evidence of God's ability to activate His freedom of choice by entering into qualitative interaction with mankind through His thinking and His reason. The prophet Isaiah was inspired to quote God as asking man to walk through the process of reasoning together with His Maker. *"Come now, let us reason together."* [96] This is the voice of a personal and dynamic God who clearly involves Himself in the moment-by-moment transitions of His creation.

So, God is a Being who uses reason – the sequential process of His perfect mind. But what of His will - His ability to choose? Referring to the story of Jonah once again, we can see the activity of God's choices as He walked through the process of bringing the people of Nineveh to accountability. *"When God saw what they did and how they turned from their evil ways, He had compassion and did not bring upon them the destruction He had threatened."* [97]

---

96   Isaiah 1:18 (NIV)
97   Jonah 3:10 (NIV)

Further evidence of God in sequence, and dynamically in relation-ship to His creation, is found in these words, *"Rend your heart and not your garments. Return to the Lord your God, for he is gracious and compassionate, slow to anger and abounding in love, and he relents from sending calamity. Who knows? He may turn and have pity and leave behind a blessing."* [98]

God's interaction with Israel gives powerful evidence of God's dy-namic and continual relationship with man. *"The people returned to ways even more corrupt than those of their fathers, following other gods and serving and worshiping them. They refused to give up their evil practices and stubborn ways. Therefore the Lord was very angry with Israel and said, "Because this nation has violated the covenant that I laid down for their forefathers and has not listened to me, I will no longer drive out before them any of the nations Joshua left when he died." The Lord had allowed those nations to remain; he did not drive them out at once by giving them into the hands of Joshua."* [99]

The picture of God watching for man's actions and responding with His own reactions is evidenced here, *"Hate evil, love good; maintain justice in the courts. Perhaps the Lord God Almighty will have mercy on the remnant of Joseph."* [100]

Jesus speaks to the Father as One who is listening and ready to re-spond to given requests, *"Father, if you are willing, take this cup from me; yet not my will, but yours be done."* [101]

No-where does it appear that Jesus was ever reacting to a pre-or-dained script. Rather, He lived in a responsive relationship with the Father who, in turn, reacted and responded to Jesus. Evidence of this is seen at the Baptism of Jesus, *"And lo a voice from heaven, saying, 'This is my beloved Son, in whom I am well pleased.'"* [102] *"And there*

---

98   Joel 2:13,14 (NIV)
99   Judges 2:18-23 (NIV)
100 Amos 5:15 (NIV)
101 Luke 22:42 (NIV)
102 Matthew 3:17 (KJV)

*was a cloud that overshadowed them: and a voice came out of the
cloud, saying, 'This is my beloved Son: hear him.'"* [103]

In these scriptures we can clearly see God's instant interaction to an
earthly situation. He was saying that He was pleased – an obvious
expression of a chosen emotion and reaction. Hardly the testimony
of inertia!

Have you ever thought about God's choices as He expresses His
emotions? God's emotions are nothing less than His chosen responses to that which His mind thinks upon. Some philosophers
have argued that God cannot be changed by the actions of mankind. This, they argue, would make God subservient to man's will
and behavior. Hardly! If the same philosopher gets a stone in his
sandal and he reacts to its presence, does that make the stone in
charge of the philosopher?

As stated earlier, God's reaction to man's earliest generations of sinfulness was profound. *'The Lord was grieved that he had made man on
the earth, and his heart was filled with pain. So the Lord said, " 'I will
wipe mankind, whom I have created, from the face of the earth--men
and animals, and creatures that move along the ground, and birds of
the air--for I am grieved that I have made them." But Noah found favor
in the eyes of the Lord.'"'* [104]

The Bible testifies to God's pleasure when he saw that Abraham was
willing to sacrifice his son Isaac in obedience to what he believed
God was asking of him. God responded to the moment. *"Do not lay
a hand on the boy,"* he said. *"Do not do anything to him. Now I know
that you fear God, because you have not withheld from me your son,
your only son."* [105]

Once more, the image of the changeless God being a person who
makes no response to the outside world is shattered by these verses,
"The LORD your God is with you, he is mighty to save. He will take

---

103 Mark 9:7 (KJV)
104 Genesis 6:6-8 (NIV)
105 Genesis 22:12 (NIV)

great delight in you, he will quiet you with his love, he will rejoice over you with singing." [106]

God's choice to withhold His anger and show compassion is clearly evident in these words: *"How can I give you up, Ephraim? How can I hand you over, Israel? How can I treat you like Admah? How can I make you like Zeboiim? My heart is changed within me; all my compassion is aroused. I will not carry out my fierce anger, nor will I turn and devastate Ephraim. For I am God, and not man - the Holy One among you. I will not come in wrath."* [107]

Are we to satisfy ourselves with the idea that verses like these are simply for the entertainment of the spiritually dull or merely to motivate mankind to think fondly of their Creator? Can man think well of a God who portrays Himself in one way, simply to cloak the reality of His real Self?

Considering these verses, we may ask, was He really merciful? Did He genuinely decide to forgive? Did He actually turn from an act of destruction? Did He really restrain His wrath, remembering and reasoning about man's fleshly inabilities? If so, He is genuinely a God in an interactive relationship with His creation, activating His will and choosing the constant best in the context of His love. If not, He is – at the very least – someone else who is not described in the Bible.

Consider the emotion expressed in these words from God, *"Then in the nations where they have been carried captive, those who escape will remember me - how I have been grieved by their adulterous hearts, which have turned away from me, and by their eyes, which have lusted after their idols. They will loathe themselves for the evil they have done and for all their detestable practices. And they will know that I am the Lord; I did not threaten in vain to bring this calamity on them."* [108]

---

106 Zephaniah 3:17 (NIV)
107 Hosea 11:8,9 (NIV)
108 Ezekiel 6:9,10 (NIV)

And, *"Who is a God like you, who pardons sin and forgives the transgression of the remnant of his inheritance? You do not stay angry forever but delight to show mercy. You will again have compassion on us; you will tread our sins underfoot and hurl all our iniquities into the depths of the sea."* [109]

God's response to sin and the raw emotion tearing at His heart is seen here: *"Because you did not remember the days of your youth but enraged me with all these things, I will surely bring down on your head what you have done," declares the Sovereign Lord. "Did you not add lewdness to all your other detestable practices?"* [110]

God's emotions are clear evidence of His chosen responses to the unfolding processes of mankind's ways. They give no evidence of a God who is beyond or outside of the succession of events we call time, but rather a God who, despite the vicissitudes of His creation is constant, unchanging, faithful and consistent. In other words, by the very activity of His free will, He shows Himself to be faithful, unchanging, and immutable.

After such evidence it is interesting to revisit the thoughts of earlier theologians and their struggles to reconcile their presuppositions, which often owed as much to their Greek roots as they did to a biblical basis.

Origen reasons, *"God only appears to be angry or joyful and only seems to repent."* [111] Once again we see a philosopher who cannot wrench himself away from his fixed presupposition, even when faced with the simplicity of God's Word.

It is my contention that God is dynamic, personal, and responsive to the changes of history and to the vicissitudes of man's soul. He exercises His will in response to circumstances. His responses are always

---

109 Micah 7:18,19 (NIV)
110 Ezekiel 16:43 (NIV)
111 Origen Contra Celcus 14:18 – John Sanders: The Openness of God p. 75 Intervarsity Press
     © 1994

consistent with His holiness, His faithfulness, His values, and His goals. His changelessness is evidenced in the consistent holiness and perfection displayed in His every action and decision. His perfection is not secure only in some form of inertness and remoteness, but is evidenced in the holy purity of His actions, reactions and decisions, which are always motivated by His perfect and unchanging love. His mind enjoys a reasoning process and is sensitive to the sinfulness of mankind and over-brimming with joy at mankind's faithfulness and love.

And from the reasoning of His perfect mind He chooses His emotional reaction, His intellectual position and – by the action of His free will - His behavioral response.

9

The "IF" Factor

IF THERE IS one word which should be underlined in your Bible it is the little word "If". It's such a simple word and yet everything turns upon it. It is the fulcrum of every relationship. In its single second of pronunciation it changes everything. It is the word that leaves us with a choice, or one of several. In biblical terms it is often used to differentiate between two alternatives; right and wrong. Because we are free, the choice is ours to make.

I began this book with a claim that we often find it convenient to blame God for the things which happen to us. Hopefully, by the time you've finished this book – if you *choose* to do so – you might have found a different approach to life, and personal responsibility.

As well as ministering in over thirty countries for almost fifty years, I have been preaching and teaching the Word of God for the last thirty years in one region of Upstate New York, so some people have heard my illustrations several times. One such example is this, "If I were to tell you that it's pouring with rain outside and that if you stay in this building you will remain dry, but you choose to walk outside, you will be drenched, would it be fair for you to deliberately walk outside, get wet, then come back in and blame me for your condition?"

Well, would it? Of course not! And yet that is how we treat God all too often. I am amazed that God has not written across the heavens, "Well I warned you!" But He is more gracious than that. He says, *"All day long I have held out my hands to a disobedient and obstinate people."* [112]

Not that this grace will be extended permanently. There will come an end to His offering of mercy. If it were not so, it would negate His integrity. Law without consequence is simply good advice! So God has often warned us by giving clear alternatives for our responses. He states, "If you do this, then this is the result, but if you don't, other consequences will occur."

It is a logical and reasonable argument that the one who chooses to ignore God's gracious warning is the one who 'creates' the consequence, not God Himself. Who then is the creator of evil?

One of my favorite "If" stories is early in the biblical narrative that tells of the first dysfunctional family. Most of us know the story of Cain and Abel, two brothers who had chosen different paths for their industry. Cain was a farmer. Abel kept flocks of animals.

At some point in their upbringing they had understood that a thanksgiving offering would be a good way of expressing worship. [113] For some reason God accepted Abel's offering, but not Cain's. This is where the 'If' conversation starts, and it proves to be a great example of discipleship training. Finish this story and you'll see that personal choices can have profound effects on you personally, on your relationships with others, with God, and even on the entire history of mankind.

God spoke to Cain. *"Why are you angry? Why is your face downcast?"* [114] At this point it is important to note that God doesn't ask questions because He doesn't know the answer. He asks questions

---

112 Romans 10:21
113 Genesis 4:3,4
114 Genesis 4:6

so that we might discover both the right question and the correct answer. Now the "If Factor" comes into play. God gives Cain some alternatives. *"If you do what is right, will you not be accepted? But if you do not do what is right, sin is crouching at your door; it desires to have you, but you must master it."* [115]

Cain was clearly given a choice and the next words of the story are devastatingly clear as to which alternative he chose, *"Now Cain said to his brother Abel, 'Let's go out to the field.' And while they were in the field, Cain attacked his brother Abel and killed him."* [116]

Do you see the full implications of this story? God Himself is saying, *"Sin is crouching at your door; it desires to have you, BUT YOU MUST MASTER IT."* Not only did Cain's choice involve making a right moral decision, it had the ability of sending the tempter packing! That is, if you believe this is actually what God was saying. Perhaps your theology has you thinking that God was just playing a game with Cain, and that he had no real choice.

I can see a clear narrative. God saw the heart of this bitter young man. His anger started some time before the actual murder of his brother, previous to the point when his offering before God appeared to be unacceptable. In fact the offering was void simply because of the condition of the young man's heart. Like any other minister, whether the ministry be that of preaching to the masses or caring for several sheep, the heart must be right before God can receive the glory. No amount of public offerings changes that.

We have already established a biblical picture of our God as being dynamically interactive with His creation. He is not an eternal blob of perfection shimmering somewhere in the unfathomable distance. He is a Person, holding, using and expressing all the attributes of personality in perfect holiness. That's what righteousness is - being perfectly related to everything, all the time - and God is righteous. [117]

115 Genesis 4:6,7
116 Genesis 4:8
117 Job 4:17

See how God makes the alternatives clear and plain in the greatest of "If" chapters, Deuteronomy, Chapter 28. The New International Version allows for eight "Ifs" in all, but it should be made clear from the start that there's a sting in the tail. They come in the form of "But if not(s)"!

The first half of the chapter begins with a list of benefits which accompany obedience. *'If you fully obey the LORD your God and carefully follow all his commands I give you today, the LORD your God will set you high above all the nations on earth. All these blessings will come upon you and accompany you if you obey the LORD your God.'* [118]

What follows is a list of the blessings in question, *"blessed in the city and blessed in the country….the fruit of your womb will be blessed, the crops of your land and the young of your … Your basket and your kneading trough* (that means your shopping cart and kitchen). *You will be blessed when you come in and blessed when you go out, enemies will be defeated, a blessing on your barns and on everything you put your hand to, your land. God will establish you as his holy people, all the peoples on earth fear you. The LORD will grant you abundant prosperity — The LORD will open the heavens, the storehouse of his bounty, you will lend to many nations but will borrow from none. The LORD will make you the head, not the tail; you will always be at the top, never at the bottom."* [119] All of this is contingent on one simple caveat, *"Do not turn aside from any of the commands I give you today, to the right or to the left, following other gods and serving them."* [120]

This would seem to be sufficient of a warning, but God goes farther. He spends the rest of the chapter describing what will take place if you do not obey His laws. It's plain speaking right from verse one: *"However, if you do not obey the LORD your God and do not carefully follow all his commands and decrees I am giving you today,*

---

118 Deuteronomy 28:1,2
119 Deuteronomy 28:3-14
120 Verse 14

all these curses will come upon you and overtake you." [121] In other words, 'It's raining outside. Stay inside and you'll remain dry. If you walk outside don't blame me. I warned you – and in some detail!'

And what detail! There are sixty-eight verses in this chapter and from verse fifteen onwards it's a description of the consequences of wrong choices! Don't skip this next section! You may just miss a description of your nation in its present day condition. There might be a picture of your kids, your business, your politics, maybe even you... If you don't mind I'll translate it for you. You can check my accuracy with the original.

- Your cities will become a cultural wilderness and your farms will become factories.
- Your shopping cart will cost more than ever before and your kitchen will be empty. It will just be a place where the consumers of your family visit from time to time to get what they want, seldom meeting or eating together.
- Kids will grow up in rebellion and everything you reproduce will turn against you.
- There will be no restful place for you because busy-ness will pervade your work and invade your home.
- There will be no escaping the demands of the outside world.
- Your hands will multi-task to the point of confusion.
- That into which you trusted your future will disappear overnight.
- New diseases will appear for which you have no answer, except that they have come about because of new behaviors you have inhabited.
- Your skies will be polluted by the clouds of your progress and the ground beneath your feet will turn to dust.
- Your enemies will rule over you. They will own you.
- Even in the mid day you will grope like a people lost in the dark.
- You will not succeed in anything. Your work will be futile.

---

121 Deuteronomy 28:15

- You will be robbed of everything, even your very identity.
- Your fondest relationships will wither and your lover will walk away to another.
- You will build a house but never own it.
- You will start a business but others will enjoy its fruit.
- Your belongings will be taken from you by force.
- Your children will be ruled and educated by those who are alien to your ways and you will have no say in their upbringing.
- Aliens will inhabit your land.
- Your history will be forgotten and you will become an object of ridicule – a proverb.
- You will work hard yet have no reward.
- Your offspring will be captivated by those who oppose you.
- Other nations will lend to you and become the owners of your land.
- They will be the head and you will be the tail.
- This will be the end of you. An enemy speaking a language you do not understand will swoop down upon you and over-take you. They will have no respect for the old or pity upon the young. [122]

I can't go on! The picture is too painful and I'm only three-quarters of the way through that awesome chapter. It finishes with these terrible words, *"There the LORD will give you an anxious mind, eyes weary with longing, and a despairing heart. You will live in constant suspense, filled with dread both night and day, never sure of your life. In the morning you will say, 'If only it were evening!' and in the evening, 'If only it were morning,' because of the terror that will fill your hearts and the sights that your eyes will see."*

If you were conscientious enough to read the last few dozen lines you will realize I took some liberty with the paraphrase. You may wish to put other emphases where you feel they belong. The simple outcome is this – God gives us alternatives. It is not that He is threatening us with curses because of our disobedience. God never curses anyone

---

122 Paraphrasing Deuteronomy 28:16-68

out of vengeance! But it *is* raining outside and he lovingly tells us how we may remain dry.

This is an important point. Many people have idea that God is sitting somewhere in heaven just waiting to punish them with some dreadful circumstance because of their most recent sin. What a terrible picture of God!

And yet there *are* such things as curses, malignant patterns recurring even over generations which keep families, clans, whole nations, under bondage. But God is a God of deliverance, a God of hope and healing.

I have often been asked, "Why did God allow me to be born into such a family? I was unwanted. We were poor. We were mistreated" and the story is often generations old. My answer is this. I believe that God graciously allows yet another child to be born into that family because each one of us, should we hear a clear expression of the good news of the gospel of Christ, will be given the opportunity to be the last in the line under the curse, and the beginning of a new inheritance under the blessing! What a privilege to have such a place in such a family!

10 | Get Real, and Listen to Your Donkey!

CHOICES! YOU WOULD think that it would be easy to choose when the alternatives are so plain, but it amazes me to see how many choose to remain in their pain, in their dysfunction, in their poverty. It is the work of the enemy to convince a person that this is their identity. 'That's how it is for your family. You've always struggled.'

Some families are so dysfunctional that crisis after crisis draws them closer. Like family members of trapped miners, they gather at the pit-head of their despair. There's great unity there. They're all in it together. They hug and empathize with one another. There is a common bond. It's who they are. But they are not miners, working hard for a living and trapped in the mine. They are just gathered around something that could have probably been avoided, such as alcoholism, an overdose, a divorce, a prison sentence, a delinquent child, unemployment. "This is who we are. We've always struggled. This is what pulls us all together." Without a crisis it's as if they have no identity, so guess how they choose to live!

I believe that people should be educated and encouraged away from this crisis oriented 'welfare mentality' and into a productive destiny. I am all for the community caring for needy people. I am moved by the statement of the first Church in history.

"There were no needy persons among them.
For from time to time those who owned lands or houses sold them,
brought the money from the sales and put it at the apostles' feet,
and it was distributed to anyone as he had need." [123]

That's a powerfully high standard set by a truly compassionate people. But I'm sure this level of compassion and genuine love in the New Testament Church was also displayed by empowering people to make right choices which lead them out of poverty and into healing.

One of the greatest testimonies to the spirit of genuine revival that accompanied the ministry of William Booth, the Founder of The Salvation Army, was the necessity to create something called "Employment Agencies", never previously in evidence. The reason for this need was the number of drunks and dead-beats who were truly converted and needed an outlet for their sense of purpose and destiny. Another of Booth's inventions was Travel Agencies, again never previously seen in the business world, but made necessary by those who chose to follow God's call on their lives by taking the gospel to the nations. This is the kind of real conversion which changes societies and brings the culture of God's kingdom to ground level.

I believe that those who cannot work should be fed, housed and cared for by the community. I also believe that those who can work, should, and should not be fed by the community without contributing to their upkeep. Paul says it quite clearly: *'For even when we were with you, we gave you this rule: "If a man will not work, he shall not eat. We hear that some among you are idle. They are not busy; they are busybodies. Such people we command and urge in the Lord Jesus Christ to settle down and earn the bread they eat. And as for you, brothers, never tire of doing what is right."* [124]

Paul was a great one for bringing reality to people and there's nothing quite like it for setting people free. A good dose of reality, usually

---

123 Acts 4:34,35
124 2 Thessalonians 3:10-13

couched in a discourse about some "Ifs" and "If not's", can lead to release and deliverance by way of some Holy Spirit-led choices.

I remember hearing of a doctor in the 1970s treating patients who had suffered terribly from the effects of drug-abuse during the 60s. You know what they say, "If you remember the 1960s you weren't really there!" Well, these clients had been 'there' and didn't remember a thing. They were in bad shape. Few of them could function at all. They were almost vegetable-like, needing to be dressed, fed and entertained. You get the picture.

The doctor had a great idea. He wondered how they would respond to a dose or two of reality, so he implemented a plan. If they rose from bed by a certain time in the morning he gave them a wooden nickel [125]. If they dressed themselves and brushed their teeth, they got another nickel or two. If they made it on time to breakfast, more nickels were distributed. So far, so good, but here comes the genius of the plan. They had to buy their food with their wooden nickels!

The transformation in the hospital ward was remarkable. Within days, clients who had previously been near to comatose were functioning with amazing alacrity. It seemed that this dose of reality had done the trick. But the doctor was finally convinced of his success when he found one of his worst patients who only a short time before had been all but helpless. He discovered him behind the filing cabinet, with a saw and a broom handle, making his own wooden nickels! Now *that* guy was cured! It's wonderful what a good dose of reality can do.

Do you recall me saying that some people complain, 'Why is God doing this to me? Why is He even allowing this to happen?' The answer is often too simple to notice.

First of all, God is not doing it. It is probably happening because of some other factor – possibly even 'You!'

---

125 For our non-American readers, a nickel is a five cent piece... and they're not made of wood!

Secondly, God may be allowing it to give you a dose of reality. Perhaps you've been living in a fantasy world, believing God for something that isn't anywhere near His will for you. I have known some people push God so hard for something they wanted, without ever asking for His mind on the subject, that He allowed them a taste of that for which they were asking, so that they might – at last – hunger after truth and reality.

Remember, God is not in a gate-crashing mode in His relationship with you. It *is* a relationship. He is showing you alternatives, helping you to envisage consequences, teaching you how to choose well and move into His blessing. But if you persist in pushing for what you want, at the cost of His best for you, He will still be loving towards you. "Oh good," you say. "If He loves me, He'll give me what I want." That is where the definition of love comes in. It's so important it deserves a place of its own in the page:

"Love is a choice to the highest good."

God will always choose lovingly. It is His very nature. His choices emanate from His character and being. God *is* love. [126] That means that whatever He causes or influences toward your life will always be for your best. It might not feel very good or look too attractive, but it will always be for your best. If you embrace it wholeheartedly, you will soon be back on track, but if you decide to push ahead, choosing your own way... well, you see we're back again at that "If Factor.

This idea of God allowing us to experience something which might seem hurtful must be seen in the context of His love, His choice toward our highest good, and our greatest benefit. At some points in history, He has allowed foolish rebels who think they know best to live through the consequences of their folly. At such times, however, He always attempts to woo them away from their foolishness, by pointing out the error of their ways. Somewhere, accompanying every folly and foible in history, there is an "If", from God. It may be

---

126 John 4:8; 4:16

in the form of a prophesy, or just a telling set of circumstances, but it is there.

The Book of Numbers might hold as much interest to the casual observer as the local phone book, but it is a great deal more than just 'numbers'. Among other things it holds one of the great stories displaying God's tendency to allow fools to go their own way, all in the loving hope of an epiphany which could bring them back to better choices.

The story is about a man called Balaam. He is an odd character. He is not a Jew but somehow he is a prophet who genuinely hears from God. The story begins when Balak was king of Moab. The king was concerned about this mass of humanity which had recently escaped slavery in Egypt and was making its way across his best grazing lands. *"They cover the face of the land and have settled next to me,"* he complained. [127] His idea was to get Balaam to curse these immigrants, *"For I know that those you bless are blessed, and those you curse are cursed."* [128]

Even though the king had sent special envoys to make this request of Balaam, as any prophet should, he spent some time before God, asking Him what to do. God was quite clear on the subject. *"Do not go with them. You must not put a curse on those people, because they are blessed."* [129]

So, that was that. Balaam made his apologies but said there was little he could do. God had spoken. Later, however, the king sent *'Other princes, more numerous and more distinguished than the first. They came to Balaam and said: "This is what Balak son of Zippor says: Do not let anything keep you from coming to me, because I will reward you handsomely and do whatever you say. Come and put a curse on these people for me."'* [130]

---

127 Numbers 22:5
128 Verse 6
129 Numbers 22:12
130 Numbers 22:15-17

Now, remember the picture. God had made it quite clear that Balaam was not to curse the Israelites, nor was he to go along with these envoys, however important they might appear and however much they might prosper his ministry in the future. After all, this *was* the *king* who had sent them and they were at his door, promising him rewards beyond his imagination.

We can imagine the thoughts racing through Balaam's mind.. "Wow, this is an answer to prayer. I've been praying for some provision for my ministry and here come these guys offering me the earth! This *must* be of God!"

Despite his secret thoughts, Balaam retained a modicum of humility. *"Even if Balak gave me his palace filled with silver and gold, I could not do anything great or small to go beyond the command of the Lord my God."* [131] Don't you love his mock humility! That mention of a palace full of treasure is really convincing, don't you think?

But then he follows up with an outrageous statement. *"Now stay here tonight as the others did, and I will find out what else the Lord will tell me."* [132] What *else!* What ELSE!? God has spoken, Balaam! Do you think for one moment that the Lord is going to say "Whoops, sorry, Balaam, I slipped up there, Buddy. I didn't realize they were going to offer you such a great reward. Go ahead and curse my people Israel."

Notice, however, what God actually said. The same God who had clearly said, *"Do not go with them,"* now said *"Since these men have come to summon you, go with them, but do only what I tell you."* [133]

Now Balaam thinks he can get what he wants. He has God's permission. Or does he? The next verse says, *"Balaam got up in the morning, saddled his donkey and went with the princes of Moab. But God was very angry when he went, and the angel of the Lord stood in the road*

131 Verse 18
132 Numbers 22:19
133 Verse 20

to oppose him." [134] Has God changed His mind on this issue, or just changed His strategy? The painful truth is that Balaam, like many of us, cannot truly hear from God. He is like us, who so often become distracted by the clutter of our own mixed motives, littering the airwaves between His voice and our hearts.

The rest of this story is both comical and disturbing. An angel from God – a fearsome being – stood in the road to stop Balaam, but the prophet drove his donkey on. After all, he was on a mission and after a reward. The donkey had more spiritual perception at this point and turned aside, only to be beaten, time and again, by the zealous prophet.

This donkey reminds me of my Border Collie. He had a matchless sense of discernment about people with spiritual problems. According to their spiritual condition, he either cared for them deeply, shepherding them constantly, or, with raised hackles, simply kept them out of the house!

Quaking with fear at the sight of the angel, Balaam's little donkey, sat down on the trail. Now I don't know if you've ever been in a horse that decides to sit down. It can be somewhat embarrassing and not a little dangerous, especially if you don't get your legs out from under before he descends to his resting place. This was Balaam's dilemma. Then the angel spoke! *"Why have you beaten your donkey these three times? I have come here to oppose you because your path is a reckless one before me. The donkey saw me and turned away from me these three times. If she had not turned away, I would certainly have killed you by now, but I would have spared her."* [135]

God does allow you to get your own way. As a last resort He will even allow you to charge ahead until it takes a major catastrophe to stop you in your tracks. And the story does not stop there. Balaam confesses his stupidity and greed and says, *"Now if you are displeased, I*

---

134 Verses 21,22
135 Numbers 22:32,33

will go back." [136] But God doesn't let him off that easily. He insists that Balaam continues on his journey to meet with the king, but only to bring the king the word of the Lord.

Tell me, which would you rather; to do what God tells you in the first place, or push ahead with your own agenda and suffer the consequences? It's always better to consider God's "If's", before they become "If not's".

---

136 Verse 34

11

It's Not 'When,' It's 'If'

EVERY CHOICE HAS a consequence, even the choice to not make a decision! Perhaps we might prefer to think that everything under the sun has its time-slot in history. How many times have I heard people who might be struggling with an addiction to nicotine, say, "I guess it's just not my time to kick the habit. When it's my time, then I'll get out of this." What comforting nonsense!

More seriously, I have often heard Christians speak of their unbelieving friends or relatives who are stubbornly resisting the gospel. The believer will philosophize upon the situation by saying "I guess it's just not his time yet. When it's his time he'll be saved."

We seldom mean very much by these statements. They are spoken out as comforting clichés. Why rock the boat by asking, "Just what do you mean by that?" Some, however, might believe that this person's salvation or their ability to kick a habit, or make some life-changing decision is out of their control and in God's hands. I've also heard it said, "God obviously doesn't want him saved right now. He must have some more things to take him through, some more lessons along the way." Onlookers nod their heads, more like bobble-head dolls than knowledgeable sages. "Well, when it's his time…"

Surely God has the ability to 'save' anyone at any time, but the fact that He is not doing so, immediately, for every lost soul on the planet, means He is either uncaring, or more to the point, there are other factors in play.

It's not a question of "When" will certain things happen, it's a question of "If" other things take place – then the 'when' will be answered. Remember, God is relational.

Consider the dramatic sweep of Second Chronicles, chapter six. What an amazing time in history! Solomon had completed the task that his father, King David, had long dreamed of. He had built a temple, an earthly dwelling place for God. At its inauguration Solomon spoke eloquently to the people and then to God and he asked God a series of questions. His basic inquiry was this: "When certain things take place, Lord, what will your response be?" In other words, "God, we've built you this place, so we hope you'll come through with your part of the bargain and look after us."

He says, *"Hear the supplications of your servant and of your people Israel when they pray toward this place. Hear from heaven, your dwelling place; and when you hear, forgive".* [137] Then that word "When" takes prominence... [138]

"When a man wrongs his neighbor and is required to take an oath... When your people Israel have sinned against you...When the heavens are shut up and there is no rain...When famine or plague comes to the land...When your people go to war against their enemies...When they sin against you — will you hear their prayer and their pleas, and uphold their cause and forgive your people, who have sinned against you?"

God responds in the next chapter by taking away the 'when' and giving a great big 'If'. God says, "When you get your 'ifs' in place, the 'when' will follow in line."

---

137 2 Chronicles 6:21
138 Verses 22-38

God wanted them to know that there are some choices to be made, not only to recompense the situation of a sinful people, but also to raise up a coming generation who would choose to walk in His ways and not depart from them.

It's like our generation saying, "Lord, when I get drunk, please look after me. When I become ill from this fast food addiction, please have mercy on me. When I distance myself from you and your people, please stay by me." But God says "If you walk in my ways and hear my voice, you can avoid the consequences of these foolish habits.

In Second Chronicles, chapter seven, God answers Solomon's prayer, with a memorable "If".

"If my people, who are called by my name, will humble themselves and pray and seek my face and turn from their wicked ways, then will I hear from heaven and will forgive their sin and will heal their land". *He continues, "As for you, if you walk before me as David your father did, and do all I command, and observe my decrees and laws, I will establish your royal throne, as I covenanted with David your father when I said, 'You shall never fail to have a man to rule over Israel."*
139

There they are; the certainties of life. God's promises are sure. They emanate out of His perfect holiness and righteousness. There need be no doubt. If I choose certain paths for my feet, God will make sure they lead straight into His blessing and protection.

As usual, just as the "If" has a consequence, the "If not" also has a result. God also warns Solomon, *"But if you turn away and forsake the decrees and commands I have given you and go off to serve other gods and worship them, then I will uproot Israel from my land, which I have given them, and will reject this temple I have consecrated for my Name. I will make it a byword and an object of ridicule among all peoples. And though this temple is now so imposing, all who pass*

139 2 Chronicles 7:14-18

by will be appalled and say, 'Why has the Lord done such a thing to this land and to this temple?' People will answer, 'Because they have forsaken the Lord, the God of their fathers, who brought them out of Egypt, and have embraced other gods, worshiping and serving them — that is why he brought all this disaster on them.'" [140]

It's wet outside and God is showing us how to stay dry. Stepping outside has consequences. We will suffer or enjoy the consequences of our choices. As Job said, *"If I have denied justice to my menservants and maidservants when they had a grievance against me, what will I do when God confronts me? What will I answer when called to account?'* [141]

The words of 2 Chronicles 7:14 have been used so many times during my years of ministry, especially to urge the church to take steps toward revival. At times of national crisis we are always more than ready to call out to God for Him to come and *'heal our land'*.

That very phrase is so soothing, so full of hope. When we look at the nations we see nothing more than the sins which individuals have chosen, but magnified millions of times over. After all, nations are only multiplied individuals. Now imagine an individual who is stricken with some sickness and hears a doctor say, "If you take these few steps, you will be healed." Who wouldn't choose to take the prescribed steps?

I began this chapter with an unusual statement: It's not "When', it's "If". In other words, don't wait for some 'Higher Power' to move the goal posts closer to your present position. Get to know from God what He delights in, what He's looking for, and why He made you in the first place. Many of your "when" questions will be answered, by what you choose in response to God's "If" statements.

The biggest 'When' question concerns the Second Coming of Christ.

---

140 Verses 19-22
141 Job 31:13,14

The disciples asked it. *"Tell us,"* they said, *"when will this happen, and what will be the sign of your coming and of the end of the age?"* [142] But what if we could conceive that there is no fixed date on some celestial calendar to which God must adhere, but several "Ifs" that must be obeyed before that great and glorious day?

What do we know about the Second Coming? Some of my friends have even claimed to know the day and date, only to be disappointed – several times. Of course, if you consider that the date might not be "appointed" in the first place, then it would be difficult to be so regularly dis-appointed.

Jesus tells us several things about His return to Earth. I find it comforting to read what He says on the subject, especially after wading through the visions of Daniel, The Book of Revelation and Ezekiel, or more to the point, after considering the various conflicting interpretations of those who tell us they understand fully what Dan, John and Zeke were on about.

So here are a few things the Word of God says about Christ's Coming:

- His coming will be sudden and quick, like the appearance of lightning [143]
- It won't be a secret, but every eye will see Him [144]
- It will be like a thief coming in the night to the unbeliever, the lost or the unprepared [145]
- But it will be something expected and welcomed by those who live in the light of obedience and readiness. Read what Paul says:

"Now, brothers, about times and dates we do not need to write to you, for you know very well that the day of the Lord will come like

---

142 Matthew 24:3
143 Matthew 24:27
144 Revelation 1:7
145 Matthew 24:43; Revelation 3:3

a thief in the night. While people are saying, 'Peace and safety,' de-struction will come on them suddenly, as labor pains on a pregnant woman, and they will not escape. But you, brothers, are not in dark-ness so that this day should surprise you like a thief. You are all sons of the light and sons of the day. We do not belong to the night or to the darkness." [146]

Let's consider a few of the "Ifs" that are involved in the timing of Christ's coming. Once more we will see that even the moment of His second advent is part of a relational interaction with the condition of the nations of this world and He is also looking for an obedient response (or otherwise) from His people, the Church.

Jesus plainly states the following: *"this gospel of the kingdom will be preached in the whole world as a testimony to all nations, and then the end will come."* [147]

This is interesting and challenging in the light of Peter's words, *"You ought to live holy and godly lives as you look forward to the day of God and speed its coming."* [148]

What do you think Peter meant when he encouraged us to *speed* the coming of the Day of The Lord? We certainly can't speed up a fixed entity which has been predestined by an immutable impassable God, but we can speed up a situation that depends upon the God who pa-tiently watches for a generation of obedient followers to fulfill the Great Commission to His satisfaction. "Then," as Jesus said, "shall the end come!"

Peter must have had this in mind in the previous verses when he said, *"The Lord is not slow in keeping his promise, as some understand slow-ness. He is patient with you, not wanting anyone to perish, but everyone to come to repentance."* [149] Did Peter really mean that God is waiting for a

146 1 Thessalonians 5:1-5
147 Matthew 24:14
148 2 Peter 3:12
149 2 Peter 3:9

certain condition, delaying His action before making a chosen response? If Scripture may be taken at face value, it would appear to be so.

Scripture speaks often of how God will patiently wait for mankind, showing grace as we stubbornly go our own way. Isaiah said, *"Hear now, you house of David! Is it not enough to try the patience of men? Will you try the patience of my God also?"* [150] Paul challenges us with, *"Or do you show contempt for the riches of his kindness, tolerance and patience, not realizing that God's kindness leads you toward repentance?"* [151] If this is real theology, then God is not sitting, twiddling His thumbs, unmoved by the vicissitudes of His creation, and simply allowing each page of a previously written novel to unfold. He is involved, and dynamically so.

Again, consider Peter's words, *"He is patient with you, not wanting anyone to perish, but everyone to come to repentance."* What a testimony to the reality of God watching over His people and awaiting certain responses, certain *choices.* In this instance He is awaiting responses from the lost, *"not wanting anyone to perish, but everyone to come to repentance."* And God is also waiting upon the obedience of the Church. *"How, then, can they call on the one they have not believed in? And how can they believe in the one of whom they have not heard? And how can they hear without someone preaching to them?"* [152] That sounds like an echo of Christ's prophecy, that the gospel will be preached to all nations, after which the Father will, decide, "Now is the time". In other words, "The time will come, if and when my people obey."

Perhaps it's time to rethink our position, sitting in our shelters, singing, *"Come, Lord Jesus, come."* It's dark outside and people are lost. Maybe we could do as God commands, by inviting as many as we can find, to come into the light. Who knows what response might come from on high!

If we choose to do so, our age might be the very time when God chooses to respond. Maranatha! Come, Lord Jesus!

150 Isaiah 7:13,14
151 Romans 2:4
152 Romans 10:14

12

Sin Is a Choice

SIN IS NOT a sickness. It isn't something that comes prepackaged in our genes. It's not in our blood and it's not passed on from generation to generation. Sin is a choice, a free moral choice. Remember, a moral being is one who knows the difference between right and wrong, and has the ability to choose between the two.

In societies which are based on Judeo-Christian values, a person is not held responsible for their actions until they have attained the 'age of accountability'. No civilized society would hold a child responsible for an action which, if committed by an adult, would be a crime. Nor would we hold an adult responsible for the same action if their abilities were impaired beyond the point of moral reasoning, unless that 'impairment' came as the result of drunkenness or drugs or the like. In that case, the consequences would be matched to that initial choice - to take the drug, or to get drunk. Then the adult would be held responsible for both that initial choice and its consequences.

At no place in the Bible are we given the impression that sin is anything more or less than a choice for which the perpetrator will be held personally responsible. The idea that sin is a physical entity, passed down through the generations in the blood, has led to many strange beliefs, not least the necessity to arrange for the Immaculate

Conception of Mary.[153] After all, if sin is in the blood in some physical form, then how can we allow it to be transmitted into the veins of the sinless Christ Child? It's seems logical, however, that if Mary must be thus conceived then so must her mother, and grandmother, and so on down the line. Was it not enough to be satisfied that Jesus was immaculately conceived?

The battle with sin is a moral battle, not a physical one. It is won or lost in the choices of humanity. Christ's sinless life was a product of His personal victory over the temptations which assailed Him daily, and not by some pre-arranged super-human state which rendered Him immune from temptation. The Bible clearly states, *"For we have not a high priest which cannot be touched with the feeling of our infirmities; but was in all points tempted like as we are, yet without sin."* [154]

Christ's temptation was clearly as real as that hurled at any of us, and the merit of His victory is in His choice to be obedient, not in some condition of immunity. Paul states, *"And being found in appearance as a man, he humbled himself and became obedient to death — even death on a cross!"* [155] In fact, it could be said that Jesus was not only tempted *"like as we are"*. It is reasonable to suggest that His temptation was far greater! Surely, if a man yields to a temptation he has not experienced its full ferocity. He has quit fighting half-way through the battle! But the One who faced all temptation, yet remained sinless, experienced what no other human ever felt; the full extent of every temptation thrown at Him, and yet without sin!

Just as disobedience is a choice, so every sin is the same. At no point does the Bible allow us to think of man as a helpless creature whose will has been rendered incapable of obedience. If man cannot obey, then how can he be guilty of disobedience? If man cannot be guilty

---

153 Roman doctrine states that the Immaculate Conception means "Mary to have been, from the first instant of her conception, by a singular grace and privilege of Almighty God, in view of the merits of Christ Jesus the Savior of Mankind, preserved free from all stain of original sin."
154 Hebrews 4:15 (KJV)
155 Philippians 2:8

of disobedience, he cannot - he should not - be judged or held accountable. If God judges man as disobedient, but man is incapable of obedience, God becomes unjust and untrustworthy. Imagine a father who orders his three-year-old son to carry a heavy 20' ladder out to the truck, then punishes the child for being unable to do it! Would you call the father "just" and "righteous?"

A great way of understanding a term such as 'sin' is to discover how it is used in Scripture. In this case, the matter is clear. Sin is to know the difference between right and wrong and choose the wrong, willfully. It is a deliberate willful refusal to do what is right.

Let's have a look at how sin is described in the Word of God. In that way we'll be able to answer the idea of whether humanity is responsible for sin, or whether the devil makes us do it, or maybe it was in our genetic makeup as a result of the fall of mankind, or even 'God planned it this way'.

In the Old Testament, sin is described as follows: To miss the mark, [156] to act perversely, [157] to transgress just authority, [158] to refuse to serve God, [159] to act treacherously, [160] to be rebellious, [161] to refuse to obey, [162] to be stubbornly disobedient, [163] to be wicked [164] to be evil, [165]

The New Testament is, of course, in agreement that sin is a freely chosen response, describing sin these ways: to miss the mark, [166] to deviate from the right path, [167] to transgress the way of truth, [168] to be

---

156 Exodus 20:20, Ezekiel 18:4, Daniel 9:5, 15
157 Exodus 34:7, Psalm 32:2,5, Daniel 9:5
158 Leviticus 16:15,16, Isaiah 1:2
159 Deuteronomy 30:17, Joshua 24:14,15
160 Joshua 7:1, Nehemiah 1:8
161 1 Samuel 2:13-15, Isaiah 1:20, Nehemiah 9:17
162 Deuteronomy 28:45, Nehemiah 9:16,17
163 Numbers 14:19, Ezra 2:3
164 1 Kings 8:47, Isaiah 57:20
165 Genesis 6:5, Psalm 7:9, 51:4, Isaiah 1:16
166 Luke 15:21, 18:13, John 16:8,9, Romans 2:12
167 Matthew 6:14,15, Romans 4:25, Ephesians 1:7
168 Matthew 15:2,3 Acts 1:25

lawless, [169] to refuse to believe or be persuaded, [170] to be unjust; to refuse to do what is right, [171] to be ungodly, [172] to be evil, wicked in heart and mind,[173].

God's response to this litany of humanity's wickedness is to call us to repentance, but some would suggest that our fallen state leaves us incapable of any good thing, but isn't obedience to God a 'good thing'? And repentance is obedience. So, are we free to repent? We might hope so!

Repentance is a choice to turn away from our present condition, show sorrow for our sin and selfishness, and begin a determined journey in the opposite direction. Or do you believe that God has already pre-ordained who will 'repent' and who will not, taking the element of free choice out of the equation, and therefore denuding repentance of any meaning or value?

We are uncovering where the great struggle of the ages takes place. It is won or lost in the place of the will. The will is the battlefield.

Some schools of thought have it that we are all born as guilty, helpless sinners, equipped only with a depraved and deficient will. So what, you might ask, would be the point of discussing any responsibility of man to respond to God's call? Some will see that call as being to some, and not to others. If that is the case, then God has preordained only some to be saved. Others believe that salvation is open to all, and a free will response is called for in obedience to God's call to repentance.

Both schools of thought are in the mainstream of classical theology and I have found it to be entirely possible for people to coexist, fellowship, and even minister together, having differing points of view.

---

169 Matthew 7:23, 2 Corinthians 6:14, 1 Timothy 2:14
170 John 3:36, Romans 2:8, 10:21, Ephesians 2:2, 5:6, Titus 1:16, 3:3, Hebrews 3:18, 4:6, 1 Peter 2:7,8, 4:17
171 Romans 1:18, 2:8, 1 Corinthians 6:9, Colossians 3:25, 1 John 1:9
172 1 Timothy 1:9, Titus 2:12, 1 Peter 4:18, Jude 15,18
173 Matthew 12:34, 15:19, John 3:19, Colossians 1:21, Hebrews 3:12

People in both groups agree that we are entirely dependent upon God's grace for our salvation. They just see some of the details of that relationship from differing viewpoints. And how!

Let's look at the idea that we are 'born sinners'. This would seem to be a pretty good introduction to a life which is predestined to failure. Talk about being born with an impediment! But if you think being born a sinner is bad enough, it's actually worse than that. We are born 'dead'!

We could start with the question, "How did sin enter the world?" It's an important question because we have all heard the argument that, "If God created everything, He must have created evil, so that makes Him less than holy." The truth is, God did not create evil, He created freedom. At a human level, choice is the initiator of good or evil.

As usual, the Bible makes it quite clear, *"sin entered the world through one man, and death through sin, and in this way death came to all men,"* [174] How did sin come into the world? Through the choice of one man, and something happened to that man which he passed on to all his offspring, among whom those who read this book are numbered.

There is a big difference between saying that we were born dead than being born sinners. One is right and the other, wrong. It all comes down to your understanding of what sin actually is, and what happened when Adam sinned.

To quote Rogers and Hammerstein, 'Let's start at the very beginning, a very good place to start'.

To begin, we must understand that the Hebrew word for breath, spirit and wind is basically the same. The word *ruwach* covers all three. So it may be understood that when God breathes, He breathes spirit. So when the *'a sound like the blowing of a violent wind came from*

---

174 Romans 5:12

heaven and filled the whole house where they were sitting,' [175] it was not a meteorological event, it was the sound of God's Spirit descending upon the disciples at the birth of the Church.

Keeping this in mind, we turn to Genesis and watch as *"the Lord God formed man of the dust of the ground, and breathed into his nostrils the breath of life; and man became a living soul."* [176] In that moment in time man became more than just a body with a soul, he became a living soul, with some part of him which elevates him from all other beings. He was now spirit, soul and body.

Now we move to the moment when God made it clear that humans are free to choose. These are among the first recorded words of God to human-kind, so note the first three words He chooses to say: *"You are free to eat from any tree in the garden; but you must not eat from the tree of the knowledge of good and evil, for when you eat of it you will surely die."* [177] In other words, God states that human-kind is created in a certain way, with abilities unknown to other beings, even the angels, and obedience is absolutely necessary for this ability to remain. The consequence of disobedience, God states, will be that something will die.

Listening to this conversation was a Fallen Angel – more about him later when we get to the 'Star Wars of Darkness & Light'. Satan appeared to the female human and immediately began to corrupt and misinterpret the situation.

He began, *"Did God really say, 'You must not eat from any tree in the garden?"* See the subtlety at play here. He knows God did not say this, but the inference is that as Eve states the reality of what God said, it will seem unreasonable. Surely if you may eat of them all but one, doesn't that seem unreasonable – illogical? What's up with that!?

The narration continued: *'The woman said to the serpent, "We may*

---

175 Acts 2:2
176 Genesis 2:7 (KJV)
177 Genesis 2:16,17

eat fruit from the trees in the garden, but God did say, 'You must not eat fruit from the tree that is in the middle of the garden, and you must not touch it, or you will die.'"

Then came the great statement of Satan: *"You will not surely die,"* [178] The inference being, 'Look at me. I disobeyed, and I'm still here!?'

But the truth is, something in Satan-Lucifer did die that day long ago and far away. And ever since, he has been decreasing and suffering the great and painful loss of his former estate. That's why he must use lies and illusion, deception and forgery to entice any following. Just like the Wizard of Oz, the curtain will one day be drawn to uncover the weakling's workshop. Like Darth Vader the helmet will be lifted only to reveal the lurid lie, the hollow husk of former splendor, which for so long had been hidden beneath the guise of greatness.

Isaiah prophesies of that day, when Lucifer will be seen for what he has become, *"Those who see you stare at you, they ponder your fate: "Is this the man who shook the earth and made kingdoms tremble."* [179]

In the same way, something essential died in humankind the day they first disobeyed. The very breath of God, their ability and existence in the spiritual realm, escaped from them. And from that day, their offspring were no longer born alive in spirit, soul and body. They were born spiritually dead. Paul writes, *"sin entered the world through one man, and death through sin, and in this way death came to all men."* [180]

So what must happen in order for this relationship to be restored between God, [181] who is spirit, and mankind, who is now merely soul and body, dead in the spirit? Man must be reborn! Life must be given back to his dead spirit.

---

178 Genesis 3:1-4
179 Isaiah 14:16
180 Romans 5:12
181 John 4:24

Jesus said, *"Flesh gives birth to flesh, but the Spirit gives birth to spirit. You should not be surprised at my saying, 'You must be born again.' The wind blows wherever it pleases. (and you know why He used the term 'wind') You hear its sound, but you cannot tell where it comes from or where it is going. So it is with everyone born of the Spirit."* [182]

We don't hear too much preaching about the moment when the apostles were born again. We hear plenty of sermons on their baptism in the Spirit in Acts, chapter two, but what about that glorious moment when their spirits were reborn? It is described for us this way by one who was there.

"On the evening of that first day of the week, when the disciples were together, with the doors locked for fear of the Jews, Jesus came and stood among them and said, 'Peace be with you!' After he said this, he showed them his hands and side. The disciples were overjoyed when they saw the Lord. Again Jesus said, 'Peace be with you! As the Father has sent me, I am sending you.' And with that he breathed on them and said, 'Receive the Holy Spirit.'" [183]

Did you notice, Jesus *breathed* on them, just as He had on Adam? And what is the New Testament word for the spirit He imparted? It's *pneuma,* which means a breath, a spirit, a current of air. The disciples were the first to be complete, once more, for the first time in the history of humanity since the moment before Adam sinned!

Without that intervention of grace, mankind is lost in his little soul and body, with no ability to live and relate in the spiritual realm. He is born that way, spiritually dead. But – to get back to our original question – is he born a 'sinner'. If so, we had better adopt the position of the priest who hurries to the bedside of a dying baby to minister baptism, to ensure that this sinner is "in the church" and on his way to Heaven!

---

182 John 3:6-8
183 John 20:19-23

No. Sin is a moral issue and as such is only the concern of moral beings; those who know the difference between right and wrong and have the ability to choose between the two. The Jews make this abundantly clear when they recognize the coming of moral accountability with the celebration of bar (or bat) mitzvah, before which, children are not held accountable in the same way an adult would be. [184] A great example of this is spoken of in the book of Isaiah: *"The virgin will be with child and will give birth to a son, and will call him Immanuel. He will eat curds and honey when he knows enough to reject the wrong and choose the right."* [185] Notice, the child would grow to a time of knowing right from wrong. And of course we know of whom Isaiah spoke!

The Early Church was quite clear on this issue, that sin is the outcome of a choice of the will of a free moral being. Let's consider the testimony from the very generation of the first churches on Earth. What they believed came directly out of the church's Jewish roots and by apostolic teaching.

Athenagorus was an Athenian philosopher who converted to Christianity. He wrote copiously, but is best known for his *'Plea for Christians'*, which he wrote in 177 A.D. He is rightly classified as one of the 'Ante-Nicene Fathers', [186] men who represented a wide spectrum of nationality, class and tongue. Their writings do not all agree on every point of doctrine but their united voices created a foundation for Christian doctrine and practice which we ignore at our peril.

Later thinkers such as Augustine, often called the father of Catholic theology, Luther and Calvin, were yet to come, the first by several generations and the latter two by more than a millennium, but these men of the ante-Nicene era, closer as they were to biblical times, demand our attention, especially in the area of their understanding of sin, the freedom of the will, and personal responsibility.

---

184 Bar is Hebrew for 'son' – Bat for 'daughter'
185 Isaiah 7:14-16
186 The Nicene Council met in AD 325 from which is derived The Nicene Confession. We call apologists before that time 'Ante' of 'before' Nicene.

Let's get back to Athenagorus. We left him hanging back there in order to give some context to his generation. What does he say about this idea of the freedom of the will, of sin being a choice and whether we are born 'sinners'?

In one of his writings he states, *"Although all human beings who die rise again, yet not all who rise again are to be judged; for if only a just judgment were the cause of the resurrection it would of course follow that those who had done neither good nor evil – namely very young children – would not rise again."* [187]

As to the idea that sin is anything other than a free moral choice, he says, *"For man is not spoken of as murder but by committing it he received the derived name murderer, without being himself murder; and to speak concisely, no other evil is a substance; but by practicing any evil it can be called evil. For a man is evil in consequence of his actions. For he is said to be evil because he is the doer of evil.'* He continues, *'I say that man was made with free will, not as if there were already some existing evil which he had the power of choosing if he wished, but the power of obeying or disobeying God is the only cause."* [188]

Other writers also give testimony to their understanding of sin being the outcome of the disobedience of free moral beings. For this quote we turn to Aristedes, a Christian apologist born late in the first Century. He published an apology for Christianity which the author presented to the Roman Emperor Hadrian, at Athens, in 126 A.D. Note these words and try to imagine a generation of Christians who would be so convinced of their faith and of God's promise of Heaven, *"And when a child has been born to one of them (speaking of Christians) they give thanks to God and if, furthermore, it happen to die in childhood, they give thanks to God the more, as to one who has passed through the world without sins."* [189]

Justin Martyr [190] addressed the subject of pre-determinism. At that time

---

187 'The Resurrection of the Dead' by Athenagorus, Chapter 14.
188 'Concerning Free Will' by Athenagorus (Date unknown)
189 'The Apology of Aristedes to Hadrian' – circa A.D. 125 to 127
190 Justin Martyr lived from 110 A.D. to 165 A.D.

many were acquainted with Greek philosophy and it had begun its encroachment into Christian thinking. To counteract this, Aristedes wrote the following, *"But neither do we affirm that it is by fate that men do what they do, or suffer what they suffer, but that each man by free choice acts rightly or sins. The Stoics, not observing this, maintained that all things take place according to the necessity of fate. But since God in the beginning made the race of men and of angels with free will, and at their own disposal, to do whatever He had strengthened each to do, made them so, that if they chose the things acceptable to Himself, He would keep them free from death and from punishment; but if they did evil, He would punish each as He sees fit."* [191]

Irenaeus was born in Syria in 120 A.D. During his time, Irenaeus was sent to Rome to correct some heresies which had begun to affect the Church. He plainly stated the Christian belief in the position of sin as being an act of a free-willed moral being when he wrote, *"And again, who are they that have been saved and received the inheritance? Those doubtless who do believe in God and who have continued in His love… and innocent children, who have no sense of evil."* [192]

Irenaeus makes the important point that this granting of the freedom of the will is significant in that it shows how God governs. His kingdom is a kingdom of relationships with character qualities expressed as they can only be – through absolute freedom to choose otherwise. He makes the point that a ruler who would force the affection of his subjects, and then calls it a relationship, not only fools them, he fools himself!

"This expression, '"How often would I have gathered… and you would not' [193] *sets forth the ancient law of human liberty because God made man a free agent from the beginning, possessing his own power even as he does his own soul, to obey the behests of God voluntarily and not by compulsion of God. For there is no coercion with God but a good will is present with Him continually. And therefore does He give good counsel to all. And with man as also in angels,*

191 'Dialogue with Trypho', Chapter LXXXVIII by Justin Martyr
192 'Against Heresies' Book IV, Chapter XXVII by Irenaeus
193 Matthew 23:37

He has placed the power of choice... so that those who had yielded obedience might justly possess what is good, given indeed by God, but preserved by themselves." [194]

It seems that these Early Church Fathers won't let us get away with anything! Even our tendency to blame God comes under their scrutiny!

Alongside such giants as Justin Martyr and Irenaeus, Clement of Alexandria is seen as a co-founder of Christian literature. He taught in the Pantaenus [195] in Alexandria which was dubbed *'the brain of Christendom',* where he taught Origen. [196] Jerome calls him *'the most learned of all the Ancients"* and Eusebius names him *'an incomparable master of Christian philosophy'.*

Clement wrote, *"God, then, is good. For the Divine Being is not angry in the way that some think; but often restrains, and always exhorts humanity, and shows what ought to be done. And God does not inflict punishment from wrath, but for the ends of justice; since it is not expedient that justice be neglected on our account. Each one of us who sins, with his own free will choose punishment and the blame lies with him who chooses. God is without blame."* [197]

In chapter seven of the same work, he writes, *"Therefore, volition* [198] *takes the precedence of all; for the intellectual power are the ministers of the will. Will, it is said, and thou shalt be able."*[199]

But surely there is more to it than just "willing" our way through life! And where is this "will"? We'd better have a look at some biblical anatomy...

---

194 'Against Heresies' Book IV, Chapter XXXVII by Irenaeus
195 The Pantaenus; a catechetical school in Alexandria, Egypt in the late 2nd Century AD
196 Origen, according to tradition, was an Egyptian. He revived the Catechetical School of Alexandria but was later expelled by Clement for being ordained without the Patriarch's permission! He relocated to Caesaria Maritima where he was tortured to death during a persecution.
197 'The Instructor' by Clement of Alexandria (153-217 AD) Chapter VIII
198 Volition = the action of the will, a choice or act of the will
199 'The Instructor', Chapter VII

13 | The Soul Train

THE OLD ADAGE 'Where there's a will there's a way', often replaced by, 'Where there's a will, there's a group of angry relatives', is now going to be changed to the question, 'Where *is* the will?'

We are created by a Trinity Person, Father, Son, and Holy Spirit. Not surprisingly, He made us in a trinity formation. We are Spirit, Soul and Body. Paul wrote, *"May God himself, the God of peace, sanctify you through and through. May your whole spirit, soul and body be kept blameless at the coming of our Lord Jesus Christ."* [200]

Within the soul there sits another dynamic trinity, the Mind, the Will, and the Emotions. Each of these has its perfect place and its own contribution. But like everything else in the kingdom of God, each part needs to learn how to stay in place, and not be allowed to step out of its proper measure of rule.

The kingdom of God is a kingdom of priorities. First things should always come first. If secondary matters are allowed to take precedence, sooner or later chaos will ensue. The priorities of God's kingdom begin with God Himself. He knows all created beings, powers and principalities. He knows they are less than He. He is Creator, they are created. It's a simple as that. He has looked around and, in His absolute wisdom,

---
200 1 Thessalonians 5:23

has decided that He is best. So He instructs us with His words, *"Hear, O Israel: The LORD our God, the LORD is one. Love the Lord your God with all your heart and with all your soul and with all your strength."* [201]

This first priority is clearly underlined with these words of Jesus, *"seek first his kingdom and his righteousness, and all these things will be given to you as well."* [202]

As soon as God established a 'first', then He also lays everything else into at least second place, and a subsidiary position to that which is 'first'. It's like this with everything He does. In God's ways there's never any doubt about what is most important, out of which all other life, health, and success, flows. He says *'Seek first'*… and all other things will assume their correct position and priority. He is clear on the matter of cutting corners. He says, *"Blind Pharisee! First clean the inside of the cup and dish, and then the outside also will be clean."* [203] *"If you are offering your gift at the altar and there remember that your brother has something against you, leave your gift there in front of the altar. First go and be reconciled to your brother."* [204] "First take the plank out of your own eye, and then you will see clearly to remove the speck from your brother's eye." *"The gospel must first be preached to all nations."* [205] It's always 'first' followed by 'then'.

As it is in all kingdom things, priorities reign in the created order, not least within our human make-up. And the line-up of priorities is accurately portrayed by the order in which we tend to list them. First, spirit, followed by the soul, then the body brings up the rear. (No pun intended).

Within the soul is another arrangement of priorities, the Mind, Will and Emotions, and boy, do we get in trouble if we mix those priorities

---

201 Deuteronomy 6:4,5
202 Matthew 6:33
203 Matthew 23:26
204 Matthew 5:23,24
205 Mark 13:10,11

and positions! At this point I would like to introduce to you a means of transportation well know by many students of Discipleship Training Schools at which I have taught over the years, "The Soul Train"!

Use your imagination, and picture an old steam train. Younger readers can make do with 'Thomas the Tank Engine'! First comes the engine, closely followed by the coal-cart (the 'tender', to English readers). After that, we have several carriages, but no ordinary carriages, they are of differing shapes and sizes, each one painted brightly, each one uniquely designed. They seem to have more dynamism than the rest of the train – at least that's what they'd like you to believe.

Now, use your mind's eye and paint some words on the sides of the train. On the engine, paint the word, 'MIND'. It is the train's place of reason and intellect, the storage place for memories and personality.

On the coal cart, write, 'WILL'. After all, it is the powerhouse. Its job is to be the fuel deposit for the engine, but it sits in a vulnerable place, open to the influence of the entities to each side of its independent position.

Lastly, here come those carriages, with all their wonderful shapes and colors. On their sides, write, 'EMOTIONS'. They are so varied and complex. They seem to take whatever shape they desire. At once calm and loving, but as the train rounds the next bend, and circumstances change, they explode in outrageous exclamations of feeling. That's their job. They are emotions.

Now my question is this, how does your train work? I mean, *first thing in the morning*, just before you get out of bed. More importantly, which end of your train is doing the pulling?

As you rise and take that first yawning, blurry-eyed gape into your day, I'll make a healthy bet that if you're anywhere near normal, your emotions will be the first to tug at your train. One carriage will probably say, *"I just don't wanna get up! Put me back to bed."* The second says, *"I feel like food, and NOT healthy mush. Gimme BACON!!"* At the same time the other emotions are pulling in several other significant directions as they recall the influences and the feelings that shaped them, either during the night, or the day before.

The critical moment comes when the train has to decide in which direction it is going to move. This, by the way, is a CHOICE. It comes by way of the coal cart – the will. But the will is not an intellectual entity. It doesn't have reason within itself. It simply fires and fuels the train as instructed by other parts which are supposed to have priority over it. Ah! There's the rub! Remember, God's kingdom is all about 'what comes first'.

What happens next is entirely up to you, and largely depends on how you have *'trained'* your life to move, and have its being. If, as I suspect, you are a human, at one time or another you have probably allowed your carriages, your emotions, to dictate the direction. *"If it feels good, do it." "How could anything that feels this good be wrong?"*

The ultimate mistake for most of us is that we actually believed that love is an emotion, whereas in reality, love is choice. Remember? *'Love is a choice to the highest good of the object of your attention'.*

If love was but a feeling, then people could easily fall out of it, like the top bunk in a cabin on a stormy sea. If love is but a feeling then no wonder people fall in it, like a ditch across the road, when we weren't paying attention!

Remember the patients in that hospital ward which I described earlier – the men who had such a shocking meeting with 'reality'? They probably started on their path to near oblivion in the drug culture through the idea of following their feelings.

The truth is simple, and should be remembered, daily, hourly. Emotions are followers, not initiators. They should never lead the way. They are

created to house reactions, to add color to right and proper deci-
sion-making, to add pleasure to righteous living. But they will just as
readily add to riotous living! After all, they don't have a mind to rely
on, unless some right choices are made, 'up-line'. They are the soul's
response to choices, one way or the other.

If the emotions, those carriages of our train, are allowed to tug us in
their direction, our train will follow along, down the line. They will
enjoy the ride for quite some time. This is what they 'feel' they were
created for. They are living life to the full. But as the train continues in
its backward direction, the emotional carriages begin to look off to the
left and the right. "Look over there, it's so beautiful." "No, over here,
this is just what I feel like doing." "I'm bored; I need us to go faster!"

All this time, the coal cart of the will is firing the train. That's what it's
there for. But a battle is going on. It seems to be running out of fuel,
but it hardly seems to matter. Fewer choices are being demanded of
it because the train has picked up such momentum that it seems to
have a life of its own.

Eventually, to no surprise of those looking on from life's sidings, as this
out-of-control train rushes by, the emotions drag the entire thing off
the tracks, and the last vehicle to plunge to its demise is the mind.

Happily, there is another way to go. It's possible, through genuine
repentance, and a submissive, teachable heart, to get the train wreck
back on the tracks again. But this time the driver needs to check the
manual. Emotions must not be allowed to decide which direction I
should go. So who leads? It must be at the other end of the train; the
mind. But even the manual says that the mind can be easily led astray.
"The mind of the sinful man is death." [206] And, "the sinful mind is hostile to God. It does not submit to God's law, nor can it do so." [207] But
there's hope! The manual also says, "but the mind controlled by the
Spirit is life and peace." [208]

206 Romans 8:6
207 Verse 7
208 Verse 6

The Word of God also warns, *"All a man's ways seem right to him, but the LORD weighs the heart."* [209] That word 'heart' seems to suggest the very core of the person. It has a link in the Hebrew to each of the parts of the soul; the mind, will and feelings. [210]

The soul needs directing, so we must add a few aspects to our imaginary train. Out in front of the engine, which is our mind, paint in a Bible, the Word of God. On the other side and in front of the Bible, imagine our spirit, standing there, strong and alert. Out ahead of our spirit, is the Holy Spirit, there to lead the way down the track.

It looks like our picture is complete, so let's see what a different journey is taken by the person who knows that their priorities are in place. I'll use myself as an example.

Many times people laugh out loud as I am preaching when I say, "You may be shy, or reserved. You might not like being with people and having to communicate; show up and do your job." Then I follow with, "That's me! I am shy and very reserved." That's when the laughter starts!. I mean, this is coming from the guy who is bouncing around the stage, 'expressing' all over the place, articulating, communicating, acting out…. He's the preacher who most of them know has been in front of thousands, sometimes millions, since his childhood! But it's true. I have never heard God articulate it, but by my circumstances, and what He has called me into and released through me, His response to my deep reservations about being with people, being in crowds, and preferring my own company, seems to have been "Tough! Get over it!"

I have never led anything but a very demanding, public life, filled with responsibility. From my teens onward, for the last fifty years, I have seldom had more than a few days at a time out of a spotlight of one kind or another. And I have known that to choose this way of life has been good and obedient, but to do it simply by the power of my

---

209 Proverbs 21:2
210 The Hebrew word leb can man 'the heart, or the feelings, or even the intellect; the center of anything. Strong's word # OT 3824

own intellect and will would have seen me crash, just as surely as the train which hurtled down the track in the opposite direction, led by feelings alone!

So what is the difference? How do we receive the power to choose rightly? We've already seen a clue; the mind controlled *by the Spirit* is life and peace. But that leads us on to our next dilemma. How can the intellect, the mind of a man, know the things of the Holy Spirit? Can spiritual things be discerned by the human mind?

It all starts with a choice: Repentance. You have the ability to stop thinking about one thing and start thinking on another. And by the way, God has blessed us, in that with all our multi-tasking, it is impossible to think of two different things at the same time! So, Paul says, *"Since, then, you have been raised with Christ, set your hearts on things above, where Christ is seated at the right hand of God. Set your minds on things above, not on earthly things."* [211]

But we are still wondering how the human mind can perceive things spiritual. Paul said, *"Those who live according to the sinful nature have their minds set on what that nature desires; but those who live in accordance with the Spirit have their minds set on what the Spirit desires."* [212] So just how do I set my mind on the things of God, and begin to understand them? Is it just an act of the will?

Certainly the will comes into play, which is first instructed by the mind, but only after the mind has had a definite encounter with something beyond even its highest accomplishment or ability.

The writer of Hebrews states, *"For the word of God is living and active. Sharper than any double-edged sword, it penetrates even to dividing soul and spirit."* [213] That's exciting! The Word of God is alive, and it has the ability of forming a bridge between the uppermost reaches of the soul, linking the limited heights of human intellect into the realm of

211 Colossians 3:1,2
212 Romans 8:5
213 Hebrews 4:12

the spirit of the person! The Word of God, by its power of revelation, draws a person's mind, and subsequently the entire soul, onward and upward, to touch, experience, and actually live, 'in the spirit!

But our spirits are little babies, younger than our physical bodies, at least on terms of their involvement with every-day life. Some of us lived for years without any spirit-life whatsoever. So how can our baby spirit learn the values of heaven? Again, the manual comes to our aid.

The Bible says, "*The Spirit himself testifies with our spirit.*" [214] God's Holy Spirit comes to speak to our spirit, in spirit-realm language, in a way that our spirit-person understands. By that means, the very mysteries of Heaven, and the kingdom of God, are unfolded into our spirit as we need them, starting with what we first need to know; who we really are!

The Spirit comes to tell us who we are by revealing who our Father is: *"Because you are sons, God sent the Spirit of his Son into our hearts, the Spirit who calls out, 'Abba.'* [215] And then we get to respond with a testimony to the Holy Spirit that we have heard Him. *"For you did not receive a spirit that makes you a slave again to fear, but you received the Spirit of sonship. And by him we cry, 'Abba, Father.'"* [216]

Here we go. Our train is moving, slowly at first, but in the right direction. Don't pay any attention to what the carriages are saying back there. They're squeaking a bit. After all, they have never moved in this direction before. Previously they fired the will to choose the wrong direction, and now the will has turned its back on them. All they hear from the rest of this new and improved train is, "Get over it, shape up, walk it off!"

Eventually, what seems to be a miracle takes place. Those emotions begin to respond to the new direction. There is a new freshness about

---

214 Romans 8:15
215 Galatians 4:6 – Abba means father, even 'Daddy'
216 Romans 8:15

their responses that they have never felt before. One profound dif-ference is this, early on, when the emotions hurtled down the track, one experience after another, it took only a little to provide a genuine high. However, as time went by, they seemed to demand more and more. But as much as they were given, the satisfaction level dropped as their appetite increased. There was a time when they could get high on so little, but then they started to gorge on feelings, only to be left empty and unfulfilled. The only answer seemed to be to go faster, and demand more, that is, until the day of the Crash.

Now, however, the emotions are beginning to respond to life, reality and truth. The slightest thing in the realm of the spirit-led life brings them to feelings they never thought possible. Now it seems to take less and less to satisfy them, and yet there's always more!

All things have become new. We have a new life, heading in a new direction, led and fed by the Holy Spirit who speaks to our spirit, di-rects our intellect by the revelation of God's word, and instructs the will to fuel in the right direction. And lastly, the emotions are not only satisfied, they are fulfilled and overwhelmed by the journey.

It certainly makes choosing a lot easier when you first choose the direction of your soul train.

14

Star wars of Darkness & Light

Long ago and far away - long before the dawning of our day,
In a land that we can only dream of,
Though it's described, so we can clearly read of it,
Lived One Who made all by Hand - surrounded by the beings of His land,
Silver beings, powerful and splendid,
Who would believe that it would ever end with 'Star Wars of Darkness & Light?'
Prepare your spirit for the fight, Children of the Day against the Night,
Star Wars of Darkness & Light.

Great Princes made by The King with authority for everything,
Gabriel, who is in Communications,
Lucifer, in Power & Creation,
Michael, the Warrior of Light, evidence of Maker's own might,
Lucifer turns from his Maker's eyes, coveting the throne for his own prize,
Star Wars of Darkness & Light; hear the words that begin the fight;
"Expel Lucifer from my sight!"
Star Wars of Darkness & Light.

Lucifer is banished from his home - in the darkness of rebellion he roams,
His shadow falls like clouds across our sky,
Upon this planet he will live or die,
The Bride of Earth is now prepared - there have been times when she was scared,
But now she knows that victory is near,
She turns her face expecting soon to hear the coming of the Prince of Light,
Great armies gathered in His sight, prepared to battle for the right in the
Star Wars of Darkness & Light. [217]

LONG BEFORE GEORGE Lucas, the creator of 'Star Wars', was on this tiny planet, and ages before C.S. Lewis and Tolkien huddled together in their tiny garret studies, as professors at Oxford University, the stories that flowed through their minds were being lived out in vivid reality.

Clive Stapes Lewis, known to his friends as Jack, is remembered for his 'Narnia' series of novels which were meant for children, but hold enough profound meaning to be embraced by all ages. He is also known for 'The Screwtape letters', an insightful depiction of correspondence from an old devil to a younger apprentice. His work, 'The Space Trilogy' is my favorite and deserves more attention than it receives.

Tolkien, for his part, is loved by those who delight in lengthy novels that lead the reader down convoluted pathways, tunnels more like, to a conclusion. As it did for Lewis, Hollywood has helped Tolkien become better known, and his masterworks, 'The Hobbit' and 'The Lord of The Rings', will live on for generations to come.

Lewis died on an historic day, but one on which he is seldom remembered or celebrated, simply because it was 22nd November, 1963,

---

217 'Star Wars of Darkness & Light' by Bill Davidson © 1978, from the album of the same name. Pilgrim Records

the day John Fitzgerald Kennedy was assassinated, a world away in Dallas, Texas. That day also saw Aldous Huxley depart this planet. Huxley was interested in parapsychology and philosophical mysticism, and was known to advocate the use of psychedelics.

Many more humans died that day, some far greater in the eyes of God, if not in the esteem of their fellow beings. But all experienced one commonality; they met, as they had never before, with the consequences of their choices. In the instant of their passing from this world to what we naively call 'the next', they all realized, in a moment, in the twinkling of an eye, in less time that it took to draw what form of breath that remains beyond the grave, that their lives had not been what they had thought, but that they had in fact been participating in a great war which had its roots planted eons before the millennia of our history; The Star War of Darkness and Light.

In chapter two, I began with these words, 'We were not the first beings ever made, nor were we the first animate moral beings God chose to create…' and I promised 'more of that later'. It's time to return to that theme.

Free Moral Beings, you will recall, are those who know the difference between right and wrong, and have the ability to choose between the two. I have attempted to establish that freedom at this level is essential to a mature relationship. Freedom, that is, to obey, comply, act righteously, or do otherwise. We have also considered that no character trait can have any value unless the actor has the ability to do other than that which we would call noble, faithful or trustworthy; in other words, he has freedom of choice.

God governs this way. The testimony of the scriptures is clear. He is One who relates to His creation in the same way He has called us to relate to each other; with grace, patience and forbearance, responding to the behavior of others with choices that reflect tolerance, grace and mercy.

Not every level of God's creation comes into this realm. In other levels of His created order God has implanted certain skills and attributes, some of which border on the incredible, and all to show His amazing complexity and beauty. However, these attributes are not a matter of choice; they are inherent in the species, placed there by the sovereign Hand of their Creator.

The Arctic Tern, who returns to the same northern nesting ground throughout its life, may spend the winter in Hawaii and makes the seasonal commute between the two without the aid of a GPS. Well, that's not quite true. She *does* own a global positioning satellite navigation system, but it's in her head!

These birds have even been seen to leave certain of their young behind on the beaches of Alaska, still making their trial runs along the sand before making their way out to sea. And when they're ready they take to their wings and head out across the ocean, guess where they go! Why, to their family's winter haven of course. Where else? But how they get there, having made no previous flights and having no adults around to show the way, nobody knows, save their Designer. And what if they do take the occasional rest stop on a Chinese freighter bound for San Francisco, taking them miles out of their way; once they are refreshed they simply take off again and unerringly recalibrate their route!

Modern science will simply fluff off such abilities as a result of millions of years of evolution. But if that is the case, why do we humans get lost on the way to the airport? And why didn't one of us decide, some millions of years ago, to learn how to fly? The invention of the airplane is pretty tame by comparison! And why, in the course of those millions of years of evolution, didn't the Terns lose their way, to the point of extinction?

The House Martin builds intricate three-storey town houses under the roof and against the wall of his human neighbor. These little guys have been taken out of their natural environment and placed in cages in science labs. For three generations they sat there, caged and unnatural. But when they were released, guess what they did. They found the nearest house and made identical homes to those built by their predecessors. No plans or history books were required. They had intuitive inherent skills, placed there by their Maker.

Take free willed moral beings out of our environment for a year or so and we become totally disoriented and return home suffering Post Traumatic Stress Disorder!

These seemingly miraculous attributes are found throughout the animal kingdom. They are signs of God's sovereignty. He has given us certain attributes, also by His sovereign design, but we are made for more than robotic responses. We are created for a more intimate relationship with our Maker.

There are several levels of creation. First of all there's the 'inanimate non-moral creation'. I haven't bothered to mention them previously – after all, what level of relationship may one have with moss? Then there's 'animate non-moral', like our neighbors the House Martins. For our part we are 'animate moral beings'. We respond not only to our inherent attributes; we are also (and mainly) free to respond through our ability to choose. That's what makes us 'moral' and a definite cut above even the family dog, intelligent and 'loving' as he may appear.

Having made mention of the family dog, let me interject with a highly controversial point about our pets. From past experience I know that I am about to offend more people in the next few lines that at any other point of theological discussion. But the truth is, our dogs and cats don't actually 'love' us. Yes, I know… I'm simply saying that out of ignorance and, yes, having met your Fido or Diddums, I would have to change my position. But the truth remains, (and I say this as being a "dog guy" and having owned the cleverest, most intelligent Border Collie of all time, with whom I had a wonderful sixteen year relationship), the fact is, he and all his kind have certain wonderful qualities inherent in them by the Hand of their Creator, which by intuition, express what we would call 'character'. But it is not theirs '*by* choice', but by nature. So, as hurtful as it might appear, I have to say that they are unable to '*love*' us, given an accurate definition of love. But they are certainly capable of acting in many wonderful and 'loving' ways. In fact, they are not showing their character, but the characteristics that their Creator chose to display in them in order to reveal Himself to us.

Now back to *our* identity, as animate moral beings. It is vitally important because the battle of the ages is fought on billions of very small battlegrounds. The cosmic struggle of all time, dramatized by Lewis and Tolkien and a thousand other authors dating back to Ancient Greece and beyond, will be won or lost in the individual space of one soul at a time, and even at the core of that soul, in the place of the will. The struggle of the ages is a battle between Darkness and Light, obedience and disobedience, loyalty or rebellion. It is a moral battle, fought between free moral beings whose destiny will depend entirely upon their choices.

It began long ago and far way. The record of these happenings appears only briefly and without a great amount of detail. Sometimes, as in the writings of Isaiah and Ezekiel, the prophetic visions of Lucifer and the battle in the heavenlies becomes intertwined with judgments against the physical enemies of God's people. But to understand the basics of what happened in that fateful season, we first need to be introduced to the main characters.

It is clear that God created an order of free moral beings at some point well before our time came. We were formed from the same matter as our planet [218] but these others were of another realm. The writer of Hebrews calls them *spirits,* [219] made of that special mix of air and energy the Greeks called *pneuma.* The composition of some other beings is unknown to us other than through brief references in Scripture.

---

218 Genesis 2:7
219 Hebrews 1:14

For instance, have we really any idea what these, our fellow worshippers of Almighty God, really look like? *'In the center, around the throne, were four living creatures, and they were covered with eyes, in front and in back. The first living creature was like a lion, the second was like an ox, the third had a face like a man, and the fourth was like a flying eagle. Each of the four living creatures had six wings and was covered with eyes all around, even under his wings. Day and night they never stop saying: "Holy, holy, holy is the Lord God Almighty, who was, and is, and is to come.'* [220]

All I can say is 'thank God they're on our side'! The King James Version does not describe them as *'living creatures'* as the New International Version has it. They just use the term *'beasts'*. The original Hebrew word says they were *'living things'*. Maybe that's as close as we can get in any of our Earthly languages.

Those *'ministering spirits'* mentioned in Hebrews are the angels, and a there's a bunch of them. Those who are on duty around God's throne number in the billions, if not the trillions of zillions; enough to make even a New York banker faint at the thought. John saw them in his vision of God's throne room. He described them as, *'many angels, numbering thousands upon thousands, and ten thousand times ten thousand. They encircled the throne and the living creatures and the elders. In a loud voice they sing: Worthy is the Lamb, who was slain, to receive power and wealth and wisdom and strength and honor and glory and praise!'* [221]

Maybe *'ten thousand times ten thousand'* doesn't sound like many to you, but the term used was more like *'myriads'*, which really refers to an indefinite number. Here's one place at least where the evangelist is being conservative in numbering the crowd!

Then there are the princes among the angels; ones marked out for special duty.

---

220 Revelation 4:6-9
221 Revelation 5:11,12

As my song implied, Gabriel is obviously in charge of the Communications Department. Twice in the Book of Daniel he is commissioned to take God's word to Daniel. In the New Testament he is dispatched to Zechariah, the father of John the Baptist. His words revealed not only his message but also his daily dwelling and context – where he comes from. *'The angel answered, "I am Gabriel. I stand in the presence of God, and I have been sent to speak to you and to tell you this good news."'* [222] He also shows up in Nazareth, announcing the coming of the Christ Child to His future surrogate mother, Mary. [223]

In the book of Daniel we learn a little more about Gabriel. There came a time when he, as head of Communications, found himself in an all-out war, needing the help of the War Department. Daniel records the event: Gabriel said, *"Do not be afraid, Daniel. Since the first day that you set your mind to gain understanding and to humble yourself before your God, your words were heard, and I have come in response to them. But the prince of the Persian kingdom resisted me twenty-one days. Then Michael, one of the chief princes, came to help me, because I was detained there with the king of Persia. Now I have come to explain to you what will happen to your people in the future, for the vision concerns a time yet to come."* [224]

'The Prince of Persia' was obviously not some young Persian aristocrat.. A Persian prince-ling would have fallen dead before the appearance of Gabriel, (see how John reacted when confronted with an angel from the same department.) [225] This Prince of Persia was none other than the Prince of the Rebellion, Lucifer himself, who, as the prophetic revelation suggests, had taken over a principality in the heavenlies over that region which is now known as Iran. Quite possibly he's still there!) More of him in a moment...

The one who came to Gabriel's assistance was not from his depart-

222 Luke 1:19,20
223 Luke 1:26
224 Daniel 10:12-14
225 Revelation 19:9,10

ment. He came from the Department of War and was none other than Michael, the commander of God's spiritual warfare. Gabriel states, *"But the prince of the Persian kingdom resisted me twenty-one days. Then Michael, one of the chief princes, came to help me, because I was detained there with the king of Persia."* [226]

Now let's turn to Lucifer! His turn had come. He must be revealed.

Like all other angels, he began his life long before we came around. The bible says he was present in the Garden and actually involved in creation. There is a graphic and revealing testimony of him, revealed by the Holy Spirit to Isaiah:

'How art thou fallen from heaven, O Lucifer, son of the morning! How art thou cut down to the ground, which didst weaken the nations! For thou hast said in thine heart, I will ascend into heaven, I will exalt my throne above the stars of God: I will sit also upon the mount of the congregation, in the sides of the north: I will ascend above the heights of the clouds; I will be like the most High. Yet thou shalt be brought down to hell, to the sides of the pit. They that see thee shall narrowly look upon thee, and consider thee, saying, Is this the man that made the earth to tremble, that did shake kingdoms; That made the world as a wilderness, and destroyed the cities thereof; that opened not the house of his prisoners? All the kings of the nations, even all of them, lie in glory, every one in his own house. But thou art cast out of thy grave like an abominable branch.' [227]

Ezekiel has a similarly revelatory vision, *'You were the model of perfection, full of wisdom and perfect in beauty. You were in Eden, the garden of God; every precious stone adorned you: ruby, topaz and emerald, chrysolite, onyx and jasper, sapphire, turquoise and beryl. Your settings and mountings were made of gold; on the day you were created they were prepared. You were anointed as a guardian cherub, for so I ordained you. You were on the holy mount of God; you*

---

226 Daniel 10:13
227 Isaiah 14:12-20

walked among the fiery stones. You were blameless in your ways from the day you were created till wickedness was found in you. Through your widespread trade you were filled with violence, and you sinned. So I drove you in disgrace from the mount of God, and I expelled you, O guardian cherub, from among the fiery stones. Your heart became proud on account of your beauty, and you corrupted your wisdom because of your splendor. So I threw you to the earth; I made a spectacle of you before kings. By your many sins and dishonest trade you have desecrated your sanctuaries. So I made a fire come out from you, and it consumed you, and I reduced you to ashes on the ground in the sight of all who were watching. All the nations who knew you are appalled at you; you have come to a horrible end and will be no more.' [228]

Isaiah is explicit in naming the demonic force he is revealing, Lucifer himself, whereas Ezekiel speaks of a nation, Tyre, and a king of that realm. But obviously the person being described is no Earthly prince. Just as in the case when Gabriel stated that he was detained by the *king of Persia,* I believe Ezekiel is revealing the principality which was dominating the Earthly realm called Tyre; no less than the same Lucifer.

To say that Lucifer was impressive, at first, is a euphemism in the extreme! He was a perfectly formed angel with a particular sphere of responsibility. He is named as an *'anointed guardian cherub'.*[229] That word *cherub* has been dealt a blow in recent history. Speak of a 'little cherub' and our minds turn to a child-like angel, the kind we have erected in stone above the graves of our children. Forget that! When humanity was expelled from Eden, God's prototype of how the planet Earth should be, He placed Cherubim [230] at the gate, with flaming swords *'flashing back and forth to guard the way to the tree of life'.* [231] No cute little baby angels here!

---

228 Ezekiel 28:12-19
229 Ezekiel 28:14
230 The plural of 'cherub'
231 Genesis 3:24

Ezekiel's description, then, is of a Guardian Angel, and this being's particular realm of responsibility was to 'cover' or hold responsibility over the design, color and even the music of the new creation. The statement *"You were there in Eden"*, present at the creation of our planet, shows he was appointed to that time and place for the outworking of his service. He is present to do his job under God's authority.

Even his appearance was a reflection of the areas of his delegated authority. Jewels were set in him, in fact *'every precious stone'*. His own beauty was to be a blueprint for how Earth would be patterned and there was more than just visual beauty present. Those words, *'Your settings and mountings'* [232] are disputed by other translations. The word *toph* is used in the Hebrew, and although the New International Version translates it as *'settings'*, *'toph'* means *'tambourine'*. The NIV continues next with the word *'sockets'*, which other translations record as *'pipes'*. This is fascinating, because it refers to a being who not only *looks* incredibly beautiful, but could even have made music as he moved. Imagine, if you can, a supremely beautiful creature, covered in every color, flashing with ornate jewelry, not worn on his fingers or around his neck, but actually in his very body. And more! Worked into that magnificent body were instruments which responded to the very wind of God. Every move he made in obedience to his Creator initiated a display of music and design; truly, the Guardian Angel of Creativity.

Then our two prophets speak of his downfall which came from the very beauty and ability God had given him. Isaiah says, *'For thou hast said in thine heart, I will ascend into heaven, I will exalt my throne above the stars of God: I will sit also upon the mount of the congregation, in the sides of the north: I will ascend above the heights of the clouds; I will be like the most High.'* [233] Ezekiel follows with, *'Through your widespread trade you were filled with violence, and you sinned. So I drove you in disgrace from the mount of God, and I expelled you,*

---

232 Ezekiel 28:13
233 Isaiah 14:14

O guardian cherub, from among the fiery stones. Your heart became proud on account of your beauty, and you corrupted your wisdom because of your splendor.' [234]

Sadly, it doesn't take much imagination for us to think of the possibility of God's gifts being traded for pride, fame and self-glory. And it isn't surprising to see how this deceptive exchange so often takes place in the area of the arts and creativity. If any show takes place, any expression of creativity, from Hollywood to the pulpits of our local churches, Lucifer sees it as his own.

He claims authority over the realm of creativity. If you don't believe me, try claiming back some area of the arts and entertainment for the glory of God, and you'll see what real spiritual warfare is all about. Not only will you get hit as you face the prince whose territory you are invading but you'll also get some arrows in the back from those behind you who, long ago, gave up on color, harmony, music, dance and drama, and any other form of creativity, and handed it all back to the Devil – good Puritans that they were!

I was blessed, however, to grow up in a denomination whose Founder, William Booth, said "Why should the devil have all the good music!" Having said that, the final tour of The Joystrings was cancelled by The Salvation Army in the United States when they saw us filmed taking our contemporary form of the gospel to the Playboy Club in London, where people actually got up and danced – to Christian music! Every good ol' boy from the Bible Belt agreed, "This abomination shall not be allowed to invade our shores!" Good Puritans that they were!

So what happened to this Prince who, through the abundance of his trade, his incredible and creative abilities, turned from God to seek his own glory?

The prophets are clear: Ezekiel says, *'So I drove you in disgrace from the mount of God, and I expelled you, O guardian cherub, from*

---

234 Ezekiel 28:17

among the fiery stones. Your heart became proud on account of your beauty, and you corrupted your wisdom because of your splendor. So I threw you to the earth; I made a spectacle of you before kings,' [235] and Isaiah begins his passage with "*How art thou fallen from heaven, O Lucifer, son of the morning!*" [236]

So began the Star Wars of Darkness & Light!

The Book of Revelation states, Rev 12:9 '*The great dragon was hurled down — that ancient serpent called the devil, or Satan, who leads the whole world astray. He was hurled to the earth and his angels with him.* [237]

Is it any wonder that Jesus calls Satan '*the prince of this world?*' [238] Given Satan's claim to own the music of the planet, is it any wonder that the wind always blows in the sad minor key? Paul says, '*We know that the whole creation has been groaning as in the pains of childbirth right up to the present time.*' [239] I have this theory, which might anger my Jewish friends, that when they at last accept the Christ as their Deliverer, one of the things they'll be delivered into is the joy of the major key!

Now back to that great war in the heavenlies?

I love the answer Jesus gave to his disciples when they returned to him, full of the flush of success after their very first foray out into ministry without him: '*The seventy-two returned with joy and said, "Lord, even the demons submit to us in your name." He replied, "I saw Satan fall like lightning from heaven."*' [240] What did Jesus mean? Was he suggesting that Satan was dislodged on the basis of this ministry campaign? Or was He delighting in the fact that the war had truly begun where it would ultimately be won?

---

235 Ezekiel 28:16
236 Isaiah 14:12
237 Revelation 12:9
238 John 12:31; 14:30; 16:11
239 Romans 8:22
240 Luke 10:17,18

Truly, He had seen Satan thrown out of Heaven. Jesus knew this. He did the throwing. They would be allowed no further access to God's dwelling. They were expelled to other regions. But that act did not end the war. At that moment in history we could well quote Winston Churchill after the amazing days of initial triumph we call The Battle of Britain. He said, "This is not the end. It is not even the beginning of the end. But we might say that it is the end of the beginning."

At this point we must consider the new species – "Human". God chose to populate the planet Earth with a species, unique in their abilities, gifted with the intrinsic desire for relationship, and therefore totally free to choose to obey Him or reject Him.

At this point we may ask the question for which we have no perfect answer: At what time in the succession of these events did Lucifer's rebellion take place? Was it before man was created, or did he see in the sweetness of the relationship between God and this newly created human, something he passionately desired? Man's response to God, in whatever he did, could be identified as nothing less than perfect worship. Now *there's* something Lucifer desired, and was ready to risk all to acquire.

However, in the midst of this beautiful and uncluttered relationship, this season of perfect worship, God knew that such freedom would inevitably lead to rebellion. Freedom always holds that probability! He knew they man would suffer an almighty onslaught from Satan and his angels, and He knew that the history of these free beings must not – in fact *could not* – be manipulated or controlled, or else it would cease to be a genuinely relational response, and the rebellious Lucifer would have every right to rise up and accuse God Himself of the inability to win, over his rebellion.

No, this victory had to be won in God's way. He would patiently woo His creation back to Himself by expressive revelations of His true being. Ultimately He would make a way of reconciliation by becoming Human Himself. In order to display His great love He would even become a substitute by taking upon Himself the punishing result of sin. By this act He would make a way back to the Father Creator for all who would believe, which means to respond, repent, entirely trust, and obey.

And there's the rub. Now we see where the war is to be fought, won, or lost. Not in the Heavenlies, with myriads of angels battling it out somewhere between Mars and Venus. They would be participants in the war, but not front line soldiers. This war would be fought in the very center of each Human, in the middle of their soul, in their will; in the battleground of their choices.

15

Choosing to Step Out in Faith

FAITH IS AN action of the will. It's a choice. Stepping out in faith is exciting. It takes a million different twists and turns. One of the reasons it is hard to describe a step of faith is that not one step is like the last one, or the one soon to come.

Of one thing I am sure, faith is not, as Kierkegaard suggested, a step into the dark. The Bible makes it clear that it is a step into the *light*. Faith is a chosen response to specific revelation which comes from the Holy Spirit. Paul makes this clear when he says, *'faith comes by hearing, and hearing by the word of God.'* [241] Faith, then, is the response to God's revealed will for us, or for some situation in which we find ourselves. I remember Kenneth Copeland saying, *"Our responsibility is to respond to His ability".*

Jean and I have taken many life-changing steps of faith in our time. Some might have looked on from the family sidelines and wondered at our sanity, but the years have proven them to be steps of genuine faith and not fancy or fiction.

Our choice to step out from ministry in the United Kingdom was a step of faith. In 1978 we had visited a number of churches in the North Eastern United States. In one of these places, hidden away in

---

241 Romans 10:17

the northern woods of the foothills of the Adirondacks, we visited a fairly new church with an intelligent and gifted young pastor.

During one of the meetings I stood praying for a line of men who had responded to a call to dedicate their lives to God. As I moved from one man to another, I heard it. Just about the closest thing to an audible voice from God as I had ever heard: *"This is your place. These are your people and this is home to you."*

Wow! I sat down after the meeting, turned to Jean and said, "We'll talk about that later." I was sure she must have heard it too. It sounded so clear to me that I thought it must have been audible to others in the room.

After some consideration we left our home and our ministry in Youth With a Mission, in England, and stepped out to the United States. We didn't move to the 'Bible Belt', where there's a large church on every corner and where it's hard to get a job if you don't belong to one of them, but to this tiny village of Lake Luzerne, NY, population 2,000, in one of the least churched areas on the entire continent.

For the first few days we lived with the young pastor and his wife. By the evening of day three, Jean and I were in bed, in tears! We both knew that something had happened since we had last met this pastor. The people were warm and welcoming, but something seemed to be lying behind the eyes of the young man who previously had become a warm and close friend. We began to think we had made an almighty mistake. But what about that clear direction? We had prayed over this move. We were sure it was God, but now it felt all wrong.

A few days later we were invited to the home of a lady who had been visiting the church in Luzerne, bringing with her a few dozen people from a larger, more prosperous area downstate a few miles.

During our visit she said, "Why don't you guys come and pastor my group down here."

"Well, for two reasons", I replied. "First of all, we're only here as visitors. We aren't legal immigrants so we can't take on a job. We're just here on a trial basis to see what God meant by the guidance we received. And secondly, I don't think [the pastor] has that idea in mind. He just said the other day that he sees the Luzerne church as a central hub and the other places as satellites."

That seemed to be the end of it. We continued what turned out to be a pleasant day. We got in our car and began to drive away from her door, when God spoke. This time it wasn't 'audible' or even close to it. It was visual. I saw a newspaper headline across my windshield. It read: "Beware this woman. She is after her pastor."

A few days later I was asked in to spend some time with the pastor. He immediately expressed disappointment in me, stating that this lady had communicated to him that I had requested to go down to her town and pastor her group of believers! I was shocked and quickly assured the pastor that it had, in fact, been quite the opposite. Then I thought it might be interesting for the pastor to hear the warning God had spoken to me as I had driven away from the lady's home. As I spoke it out, he visibly shrank back in his chair.

I don't recall the rest of the meeting, but a few days later we received a phone call stating that the pastor had warned people about me, stating that I was a false prophet and a false teacher and that people should steer clear. And, for the most part, they did.

We were devastated. Here we were, three thousand miles from home, with a six and eight year-old in tow, with no ministry, no money and just about no friends. This is the result of faith!?

At least I had some YWAM [242] schools to turn to, so I could take a week's teaching schedule and feel that somehow I was contributing to the kingdom. The director of the YWAM base in Concord, New Hampshire, told me that a local pastor communicated to him that

---

242 Youth With a Mission

he had mentioned YWAM in a time of preaching at a nearby conference. He said that after finishing his ministry, the young pastor from Luzerne had approached him and said, "Beware this man. He is out to break down the Body of Christ!" With that he pulled a picture of me from his pocket! Surely such devotion to duty had not been seen in America since the 1950s, during the days of Senator Joe McCarthy's purge of suspected Communists from public life!

It was a year later, after we had retreated out and away from "our place, our people and our home", as God had described it, that we found ourselves leading a YWAM Discipleship Training School in Ontario, Canada. We loved our time in Canada. The people on base were great friends and we liked the coziness of Canadian culture – sort of halfway back to Britain.

In this school were two young ladies from the church in Lake Luzerne. One day, during the mid-morning coffee break from lectures, one of the girls came to find me. She had been crying.
"It's our pastor", she said. "He has divorced his wife and is in a relationship with one of the women in the church. The whole church is splitting over.it."

I didn't need to know which lady we were talking about. All indications were that the relationship might have begun some time before the day I naively gave him my warning in his office. How was I to know that she was not only 'after' her pastor, she probably already had him!

Once a month we started commuting the three hundred miles from Ontario back to Luzerne. We met with a few hurting people. Dozens of others had been scattered to the wind. Two new 'churches' had started up from the scattering, neither of which exist today. We met in the basement of the house where we were staying and gradually things grew stronger. Eventually we bought the building in which God had spoken to me that night, just a couple of years before, and ever since then, Church of The Nations, Lake Luzerne, NY., has been a center for ministry and a point of influence to many nations around the world.

The King's School, of which my daughter Kellie Girling is now the principal, was founded a year after the church was formed. In the year of the publication of this book, COTN will celebrate its thirtieth anniversary, and King's its twenty-eighth. Abundant Life Church of Saratoga Springs, numbering in the hundreds, was planted out of the original root in 1986. We founded First Church of Granville in 1990, and Iglesia Oasis in Bogotá at the same time, together with La Esperanza Children's Foundation, also in Colombia. Abiding Life Church, an outgrowth of Saratoga Abundant Life is active in nearby South Glens Falls. In 1995, Church of The King was founded, where we now pastor. The Service Corps and several ministry schools have operated out of that root. We regularly support and give encouragement and guidance to literally hundreds of pastors throughout the world - and all from a step of faith that had once appeared to be a step of folly.

That was an incredible journey for us, especially in those earliest years. Church planting means 'starting again from scratch'. No pay, no congregation, no denominational resources; just Jean, me, the kids, a few friends and an acoustic guitar. We did it all again in 1995 as Church of The King was launched. This time we had with us some old friends from the UK, Roger and Doreen Brown, who also knew a thing or two about stepping out in faith.

All it takes is a step of faith, or more correctly, all it takes is hearing from God. After that, the step is simply obedience to His revealed will. The challenge is this; He seldom gives all the details. His end is to see what is in our hearts, not what He can get done through us.

Remember, He's a relational God, but don't think for one minute that He desperately needs His human relatives to do things for Him. His sovereignty can take care of that, any time He chooses to intervene. He is most interested in allowing us to win the war in the heavenlies by surrendering our will to His purposes. That, my friends, is the victory He is looking for and the choice which Satan cannot abide.

That response – the choice of obedient faith – comes not only from hearing from God, but from knowing Him. When it comes to spiritual warfare – that war of darkness against light – we are told clearly what the enemy's strategy is. Paul describes it this way: *'our struggle is not against flesh and blood, but against the rulers, against the authorities, against the powers of this dark world and against the spiritual forces of evil in the heavenly realms.'* [243]

Then he tells us what the real goal of the conflict is by showing where Satan will attack. Know your enemy by revealing his point of attack. In that, he will reveal his every intention. *'The weapons we fight with are not the weapons of the world. On the contrary, they have divine power to demolish strongholds. We demolish arguments and every pretension that sets itself up against the knowledge of God.'* [244]

After all the grand language of warfare and a description of our weaponry, Paul states that the enemy's target is *'arguments and every pretension that sets itself up against the knowledge of God.'*

Satan knows that he can win if only he holds us back from a clear understanding of who God really is. He is terrified of this world's population ever getting a clear understanding of God's true nature, His benevolence, His compassion and – especially – that He is a relational and loving Person, who is waiting patiently for our obedient response.

In a nutshell, Satan knows that whatever we truly know about God, we will love, and that this love will provoke a response, a choice, to surrender to Him and His rights over our lives.

That's the whole point of our existence. That's the war for which we

---

243 Ephesians 6:12,13
244 2 Corinthians 10:4,5

were created. That's why there is *'more rejoicing in heaven over one sinner who repents than over ninety-nine righteous persons who do not need to repent.'* [245] And that's not just 'personal salvation' – which is significant enough – it is more. It is a single victory which is counted in to the great war in the heavenlies. We win this war one soul – one ultimate choice - at a time.

The knowledge of God is the main target of the enemy. Do you recall that time when the disciples were ferrying Jesus over to the 'other side' and a storm came up on the Galilee? Our family has slept in a small hut on a beach on that very shore. Halfway through the night the little curtains which covered the open windows stood straight out, horizontally! A wind had come from some distant desert and rushed through that valley in between the mountains where the Sea of Galilee lies. And so it was that night when the disciples were on board, with Jesus *'in the stern, asleep on a cushion'.*

Mark tells the story, probably not from personal experience, as he was but a boy at the time, but as told by the disciples, later. *"The disciples woke [Jesus] and said to him, 'Teacher, don't you care if we drown?' He got up, rebuked the wind and said to the waves, 'Quiet! Be still!' Then the wind died down and it was completely calm. He said to his disciples, 'Why are you so afraid? Do you still have no faith?'"* [246]

Did you see that? He challenged them for having no faith. The reason for that, however, shows up in the next verse. *"They were terrified and asked each other, 'Who is this? Even the wind and the waves obey him!'"* [247]

Obviously those were early days. The disciples didn't yet realize with whom they were dealing. This was God on that cushion! God was in their boat! To Him the storm was but in a tea-cup over which He could place His hand at any given moment to be quieted as He chose. What He would look for in future days was a group of guys who knew

245 Luke 15:7
246 Mark 4:38-40
247 Verse 41

Him well enough to stand in His authority, step out in faith, and speak to the wind!

The only reason we were able to press ahead after our initial experience in New York was that we knew, in our spirits, that God had spoken. I cannot fully express how grateful I am to have had Jean by my side at such times. It is no small thing for a woman to step out, with young children in tow, and make a home out of a suitcase, anywhere the Lord leads, from a tent in Egypt, behind the Iron Curtain, or on the shores of the Galilee. Jean would have been an amazing woman, with or without me. I think you can tell which I have preferred!

The key was that we had learned so much over the years about God's character. We were sure that *'The one who calls you is faithful and he will do it.'* [248] We believed in the character of the One who said to Isaiah, *"so is my word that goes out from my mouth: It will not return to me empty, but will accomplish what I desire and achieve the purpose for which I sent it."* [249]

I admit, however, that at times it was difficult to believe for the next verses which say, *"You will go out in joy and be led forth in peace; the mountains and hills will burst into song before you, and all the trees of the field will clap their hands. Instead of the thorn bush will grow the pine tree, and instead of briers the myrtle will grow. This will be for the Lord's renown, for an everlasting sign."* [250]

It would have been easier at times to simply pack our bags and return home, with our tails between our legs, easier to forget the 'word' we had heard. I reverted now and then to my upbringing on the streets of Liverpool and savored the thought of a good punch-up with that young pastor! There's a thing called a "Liverpool Kiss", delivered with one's forehead to the nose of the opposition. I must quickly add that I asked forgiveness – many times – for such an immature yet delicious thought!

---

248 1 Thessalonians 5:24
249 Isaiah 55:11
250 Isaiah 55:12,13

But now these thirty years later, considering the thousands who have come into God's kingdom, the nations whose doors have been opened to us, the lives which have been transformed, and the generations of leaders who have been sent out and established in ministries and places of responsibility, it's easy to look back and see how faithful God has been. But the step of faith comes well before all that. It comes at the moment of the battle, the moment of the choice. Do I obey or do I go my own way? Do I trust what He has said, and that His character is unfailing? It's a choice.

16

Ja Wanna?

I STATED EARLIER that each step of faith has its own set of circumstances. Each can feel entirely different from any other step at some
other time. There are times when we are called upon to make life-
changing decisions which will be seen by everyone. Our move from
one continent to another was such a time. There are other times when
the decision may be made in the quiet of your own soul, where no-one
witnesses the battle raging within. Only you, and God, and perhaps
one or two others who walk through it with you are even aware there
is a struggle going on. However, the battle is no less intense, and the
victory no less wonderful.

I began our discussion with the notion that we all tend toward fatalism at some point or another. "God, do it to me" we say, or "Do it for
me." But he looks for a personal, relational response; a choice. He's a
relational God who works through that choice called faith.

Such was the situation when I began to walk in the things of the
Holy Spirit. I had been brought up in a good, sound, evangelical society. My Sunday School classes had brought me to a healthy overall
knowledge of the scriptures. I knew of the characters of the Bible and
their individual stories. Most importantly I knew the ins and outs of
the gospel. But I had little or no idea of the work of the Holy Spirit,

other than that which I had been told of His work in convicting the sinner and sanctifying the believer.

Like all who came from a good Wesleyan heritage, we Salvationists believed in the 'Second Blessing', often called 'Full Salvation', although I'm not quite sure what merit 'partial salvation' would have! These were the terms used by the heroes of the early days of The Salvation Army as they witnessed the power of God's Spirit falling in a way which, to my reading of Christian history, has seldom if ever been surpassed in nation-changing reformation.

So great was the move of God's Spirit in the earliest days of The Army that I am quite secure in the idea that the period of the Army's birth was God's time to release the work of His Spirit in the world, but because of some reservations as to the outworking and manifestations so often associated with these times of revival, and especially those reservations expressed by the Quaker in the midst, Catherine Booth herself, the world had to wait another generation for the Pentecostal Churches to be born.

Move forward another century and meet a long-haired Salvation Army officer, Captain Bill Davidson, at the end of eleven years of the birth pangs of contemporary Christian music. [251] I was also near the end of my rope and had almost hung myself. After a phenomenal start to ministry, I found myself spiritually empty and emotionally bankrupt. Jean and I were appointed to move to Newark at the very cross roads of ancient England. More of the story of what took place in that great old town can be found in my book, 'Marked for Life'.

In the first few months of our new residence I moved from being deeply frustrated, to seeing some light at the end of my tunnel. I began re-reading the New Testament and became convinced, as I moved through the book of Acts, that nothing less than genuine New Testament Christianity would ever satisfy me. I wanted it all, all the power that had transformed a team of frightened, abandoned

251 Read more of this period of Bill's life in 'Marked for Life' by Bill Davidson

beginners, into world-changing apostles. I not only wanted it, I desperately needed it!

At this time, in the midst of all that God was saying to me, I spoke back. For a start, I wanted all the fullness of the power of the Holy Spirit; that same baptism of power that had given birth to the Church at Pentecost, but (with all due respect to my Pentecostal friends) I had seen nothing up to that point that convinced me that whereas the Pentecostal denominations had once had something, they had somehow lost a lot of it along the way. Just as I believed we in The Salvation Army had lost contact with the initial outpouring of power in William Booth's day, so I felt that the Pentecostals had done the same to Pentecost. We both knew how to sing the songs about Calvary, (The Army) and Pentecost, (the other guys) but somehow we lacked the power thereof.

So I made a deal with God. I literally said this to Him. "Jesus, I know You are the baptizer in the Holy Spirit, but I would like you to find someone who will come and lay hands on me. But he must be from a Salvation Army background. He has to have been to the same ministry college as I, and understands where I'm coming from."

This, I felt, was well nigh impossible. Although thousands of Salvationists have, since those days, enjoyed the fullness of the Spirit, at that time I felt I was alone, but sill I made my bargain with God. He was going to send "My Man" to me, a 'fact' that I told my church members. From time to time they would ask me, "Has your man arrived yet?"

It took a year before I received a phone call that "an Australian" was in town and looking for me, Tony Fitzgerald, by name.

After a day or two having made no contact, we managed to get together. I invited him to our home and we sat drinking coffee (made with hot milk, English style). Tony explained that he had come to England to meet up with a man who was working the streets of London, bringing the Word of God and practical help to drug addicts. Tony's ministry back in Australia was similar, and he felt he could learn something from this more experienced individual.

On the last lap of his flight to England, Tony felt that God was telling him to make contact with Bill Davidson. His sister had met Jean and me some years before, so the name didn't come 'out of the blue', but it seemed to Tony to be 'of God'.

He explained that he had been disappointed to find that his original host, an evangelist called Vic Ramsey, had moved from London's mean streets to the quiet of Newark in Nottinghamshire. Tony and Ian Spencer, his traveling companion, also from Down Under, boarded a train bound for Newark. Upon alighting, they were met by their host. Not twenty yards down the road outside the station, Vic turned to the two Australians and said, "You know, there's a Salvation Army officer in town called Bill Davidson. You ought to meet him." Tony, Ian, and Vic all knew a thing or two about taking steps of faith!

So Tony and his mate eventually arrived in our living room in Newark. As he described his background, I realized that God had brought "my man" twelve thousand miles, just for me. Perhaps Tony was the only one who fit all the qualifications. He did indeed have a Salvation Army background and he was spirit-filled. He had indeed attended the same college as I, only his 'William Booth College' was in Melbourne, Australia, while mine sat twelve thousand miles to the north, in London. But the name remained the same!

After a few days the time came for Tony and Ian to sit with Jean and me, to talk about the baptism of the Holy Spirit. Eventually Ian found himself alone with me in our dining room.

At this point I need to explain that I had already envisioned how I would personally meet with the Holy Spirit. I had it all planned. I would have a really dramatic experience. By now I had been to one or two Charismatic meetings so I wanted the 'works', nothing less than a 'swinging from the chandeliers' experience. And I had a pre-conceived idea that someone significant would be the one to pray for me. Now if Tony might not have seen himself as 'significant' at this time, then all the less for his companion, Ian. With all due respect, he was a rough and ready type of guy. A fair dinkum Okker! No polish, no airs or graces, a typical Aussie, which, in my book, is a compliment! But what God had in store for me through his agent, Ian, was not the way I saw it happening.

He sat at the table with me, reached over and laid his big hand on my head. "Oh Lord," he drawled, "I pray that you baptize my brother in the Holy Spirit, Amen!"

I had my eyes closed, like a good evangelical should at times like these, and I was waiting for more. But nothing else came out of his mouth.

"That's it!?" I thought. "That's all he's got?" Frankly I felt somewhat insulted. Maybe if I waited a little longer at least Tony might come back in the room to rescue the situation. But no, it was just Ian and me, or, as I would later discover, 'Spence' had brought Jesus along for the ride.

I waited a respectful moment or two before opening my eyes and as I did I received a shock. "Someone's redecorated the room!" I said. Everything, I mean *everything* was brighter; the wallpaper, the paint….. everything. "Ay-min, mate" was all Ian could say, with a broad grin on his face.

After a few seconds Ian gave me a profound lesson in theology and the life of faith. He had laid hands on me, fully expecting me to be filled with the power of the Holy Spirit and to receive the gifts of the Spirit. To him it was that simple. No-one had told him to give me a scalp massage, (I've had a few of those), or knock me over, blow in my face or scream "Speak it out, speak it out" in my left ear. All he did say was, "Bill, have you got anything against speaking in tongues?"

"No," I replied quickly. Now, for a Salvationist that was quite an admission. "I have read all the books and I believe the gifts are for today." Big of me, wasn't it! Then Professor Spencer gave that lesson in theology. He smiled and said, "Ja wanna?"

Now, to those who have not had the pleasure of becoming acquainted with the English language as spoken in the Big Place Down Under, "Ja wanna?" means "would you care to?" or "If it isn't too much trouble, perhaps you might consider making this your preference." But for now it was "Ja wanna?"

"Yes" I said. And then I received my theological lesson in taking steps of faith.

"Go on, then." He said................. So I did!

I realized in that moment that God had used this big-hearted Australian, in the simplicity of his approach to his wonderful Savior, whom he obviously loved so much. In an instant Jesus spoke to me. "You've had enough experiences to last several lifetimes. It's time for you to learn to obey me without a single shred of evidence, other than my Word, my Promise, and my Character." And that's what I've been choosing to do, ever since. It's called 'stepping out in faith'... and it's a choice.

17 | Authority - Who's in Charge Here?

God's will is not always being done. For instance, He would have hoped that *all* would come to repentance, not just a few. As His word says, *'The Lord is not slow in keeping his promise, as some understand slowness. He is patient with you, not wanting anyone to perish, but everyone to come to repentance.'* [252] But this rebellion does not stop Him in His tracks, nor deny Him any of His abilities. The only ones 'stopped' by sin are those who, by their own stupidity, keep themselves from fellowship with God.

Some believe that God's sovereignty extends only to the matter of man's salvation. In other words, all of creation, including mankind, is free to carry on its merry way, but in the matter of who gets into Heaven, then God decides. And yet when we consider the massive complexity of what causes or influences a single human decision, it would seem that God would have to pluck out the individuals of His choosing in such an arbitrary manner, making it anything but typical of the God of the Bible.

It is incredible to see the interaction of one part of creation with another and the influence some sections can have on others. It reminds me of the 'Butterfly Effect'. Perhaps you have heard of the idea of sensitive dependence on initial conditions in the 'chaos theory'. It

---

252 2 Peter 3:9

suggests that there may not be such *chaos* after all. The idea is that one action causes a reaction, a change in the circumstances surrounding another set of circumstances, and in turn, these circumstances cause a change in others sets – and so it goes on until the entire environment has suffered a change. In essence, the single flap of an Asian butterfly's wings may end up creating the environment for a hurricane in the Atlantic. It sounds outrageous, but there is some strong science behind it.

So if God is sovreignly in charge of great events – and there is none greater than the salvation of an individual human being – then He must be equally in charge of the slightest event, however inconsequential it might seem. But how ludicrous it is to consider the God of all eternity, deciding, before the foundation of the earth, just who would win every game of Monopoly, or every Little League encounter. I believe, therefore, we have only one of two choices; to either believe He is responsible for absolutely everything, or that He sovreignly allows us to write our destiny by the choices of our human souls. That's another way of describing 'freedom'.

This latter position brings us back to the great Star Wars of Darkness & Light.

The epic battles shown in the movie versions of "Lord of the Rings", with thousands of soldiers on horseback screaming down the mountainside towards the forces of evil, are exciting to watch. They cause the blood of this Christian warrior to literally race in my veins (and my Scottish blood, too!). It's the same when I watch the children of Narnia taking up their royal destiny and fighting the Ice Queen. But the greatest epic takes place not on some vast battlefield, but in the secret of every human soul. It is won or lost by the choices made therein.

So, who's in charge here? Who has the authority? Have you ever considered whether or not Satan has any real authority? It's a great question to ask, because it reveals something about which few believers take much notice; that he has no legitimate authority other than that given him by those to whom it was granted in the first place. He is simply a usurper.

If you want proof of this, the devil himself gives it. It happened during a conversation which took place on perhaps the most significant battlefield ever translated into human language, the confrontation between Satan and the one who had cast him out of Heaven.

Lucifer is depicted proudly showing the Christ around his earthly domain. We can imagine Satan thinking, "How dare this God of the heavens think that by becoming a man He can grab this planet back from me! Has He forgotten that all the men are mine?"

To prove his point, 'The devil led [Jesus] up to a high place and showed him in an instant all the kingdoms of the world. And he said to him, "I will give you all their authority and splendor, for it has been given to me, and I can give it to anyone I want to."' [253]

What a fool! Had he not heard of the proverb, 'Pride goes before destruction, a haughty spirit before a fall?' [254] But still he allowed us this glimpse into his vulnerability. Did you notice it? Satan clearly stated in these few words that he has no authority of his own, and that the authority he claimed was not his, by right. It belonged to someone else – another species!

If this had been a moment in The Second World War it would have been equal to Hitler sending Churchill, Eisenhower and Stalin the keys to his war room in Berlin! Here is Satan confessing his lack of legitimate authority. What he had was only his by subterfuge. All's fair in love and war! So, of what authority are we speaking, and when did it get handed over to this usurper?

In the Book of Genesis we clearly hear God stating, 'let them [Human] rule over the fish of the sea and the birds of the air, over the livestock,

---

253 Luke 4:5,6
254 Proverbs 16:18

over all the earth, and over all the creatures that move along the ground." … God blessed them and said to them, "Be fruitful and increase in number; fill the earth and subdue it. Rule over the fish of the sea and the birds of the air and over every living creature that moves on the ground."' [255]

This is a clear delegation of authority and it is that authority which Adam handed over to a rebellious angel, that day in God's prototype of Earth we call Eden. Ever since then, Satan has been *'The Prince of This World',* although he was never created as such. [256]

Humanity had squandered their place of authority to the rebel himself. Satan knew that if God could be allowed to woo this human life-form to freely choose to love Him, even in the face of Satan's onslaught, then his own claims to authority and power would be lost. He also knew that if God had simply created a race of automatons, who robotically responded to His every whim, then God would be the loser. This was a war over free obedience, or disobedience, not about who could make their dolls act nicely. A race of robots would allow Satan to claim God's impotence and justifiably maintain that the rebellion had the eternal upper hand.

But God chose otherwise. He declared war on that moral battlefield between obedience and rebellion in the best possible way, through humanity, this second species of free moral beings. Knowing that the inevitable result of man's freedom would bring about an eventual rebellion, God made a choice before the first human was created. He planned, at a given time in their history, that He would incarnate Himself, bringing about a gift of amazing grace. We call it 'The Atonement'. *'He was chosen before the creation of the world, but was revealed in these last times for your sake.'* [257]

---

255 Genesis 1:26-28
256 John 12:31; 14:30; 16:11
257 1 Peter 1:19,20

18 | God's Choice - The Atonement

THIS 'ATONEMENT', MODELED for centuries by the rituals God had taught the Jewish people, was the key to the battle between darkness and light and the foundation of the victory.

It is a moral battle. The arguments are legal matters about who can rightly claim the throne. God's created order of humans had chosen rebellion. The authority God delegated to them had been handed over to Satan. The incarnation – the putting on of flesh – was God's next step. He would come, and in one great act defeat the power of Satan over mankind, making a way for full reconciliation.

Satan knew there was no legal way in which God could arbitrarily forgive man's sin without breaking His own law and denying the very foundation of justice. Why should he? He hadn't forgiven the angels' rebellion or Satan's own. So the lawyer in Satan comes to the fore…

Satan's case was clear: How can God, whose throne is based both on justice and mercy,[258] show one, without denying the other? Can a God of justice forgive arbitrarily, without forfeiting His justice? Can a God of mercy condemn a rebel, without forfeiting His mercy? Satan must have relished this confrontation. Little did He know the extent of the plan conceived with the Heart of the Trinity!

258 Psalm 89:14

Even had Satan heard the words, *'if, by the trespass of the one man, death reigned through that one man, how much more will those who receive God's abundant provision of grace and of the gift of righteousness reign in life through the one man, Jesus Christ',* [259] he might still have shouted "Objection!" from the bench. "The result of sin is death" he would bellow. "You have said it yourself. Grace breaks the Law!" Then, pointing a crooked finger at humanity in the dock he would end with a flourish, "I demand that they be sentenced, and that you vacate the throne!"

Satan knew that *'all have sinned and fall short of the glory of God,'* [260] He could have written it as eloquently as Paul. So from where could any redemption come which satisfies both justice and mercy?

Then Jesus came. Not as a vengeful rider on a great White Horse (that will come soon enough) but as a man, truly and properly human, while still truly and properly divine. He would live a life of loving obedience to His Father, and die to take upon Himself the due penalty of humanity – death itself. Although He would never know sin, He would become sin, for the sake of every sinner. *'God made him who had no sin to be sin for us, so that in him we might become the righteousness of God.'* [261] Blameless, He would offer Himself as God's Lamb of the Atonement, a substitutionary sacrifice. In so doing He would satisfy both God's justice and His mercy. The law of sin and death was satisfied, while the expression of mercy and grace was fulfilled.

Isaiah prophesied, *'He was pierced for our transgressions, he was crushed for our iniquities; the punishment that brought us peace was upon him, and by his wounds we are healed.'* [262]

By this monumental act of grace, God made a way for humanity to rise from its place of defeat, to stand, once more, in its place of destiny and purpose, and we would do it, one of us at a time, by making 'The Ultimate Choice'.

---

259 Romans 5:17
260 Romans 3:23
261 2 Corinthians 5:21
262 Isaiah 53:5

19 | Our Choice - Repent and Be Reconciled

All this is from God, who reconciled us to himself through Christ
and gave us the ministry of reconciliation: that God was reconciling
the world to himself in Christ, not counting men's sins against them.
And he has committed to us the message of reconciliation.
We are therefore Christ's ambassadors,
as though God were making his appeal through us.
We implore you on Christ's behalf: Be reconciled to God. [263]

TO BE RECONCILED to God is serious business. There are hard choices to be made here, not only by God, but also by us. This battle is a matter of the will, but before you think I am advocating the idea that by the strength of our will alone we might be saved, let me make things clear.

The will is not enough. We cannot will ourselves from spiritual death to being born again. And in such death we have not the capacity to make right choices and live a righteous life. Even after spiritual re-birth it takes more than our will and our understanding to walk a straight path. We are saved, and we continue on, by grace.

That word grace holds within it everything we need. It means both an underserved favor, beyond our merit, and owing nothing to our

---

263 2 Corinthians 5:18-20

choices. But it is also means an empowering gift, an enabling ability [264] to *'live a life worthy of the calling you have received,* [265] so we may, *'whatever happens, conduct [ourselves] in a manner worthy of the gospel of Christ.*[266] Could this be any clearer than in Paul's words to Titus? *'For the grace of God that brings salvation has appeared to all men. It teaches us to say "No" to ungodliness and worldly passions, and to live self-controlled, upright and godly lives in this present age.'* [267] It is not too simplistic to say that God's enabling, by His wonderful grace, is simply the power to choose what is right, and refuse what is wrong. That's discipleship, in a nut shell!

That empowering of the Holy Spirit comes after we have made an initial decision, the choice to repent. Jesus warned a crowd of Galileans, *"But unless you repent, you too will all perish. Or those eighteen who died when the tower in Siloam fell on them — do you think they were more guilty than all the others living in Jerusalem? I tell you, no! But unless you repent, you too will all perish."* [268] When Jesus says it once, it's enough. When He says it twice, perhaps we should listen!

'Repent' was the first recorded word of His ministry: *"Repent, for the kingdom of heaven is near."* [269] Before that, Matthew only records Him speaking in public to John the Baptist, and Satan! But the first words of His call to humanity involved an action of the will. Why not? That's where the rebellion began. That's where mankind had become lost, and He was here *'to seek and to save what was lost.'* [270]

The call to repentance runs throughout Scripture. It means *to think differently* [271] or *reconsider*; to feel a *moral compunction*, which leads to a *reversal of direction and action.* [272] In the Old Testament it is

---

264 Charis or charisma - a gift or endowment, an act of grace; Strong's NY words No. 5486
265 Ephesians 4:1,2
266 Philippians 1:27
267 Titus 2:11,12
268 Luke 13:3-5
269 Matthew 4:17
270 Luke 19:10
271 Matanoeo; See Strong's NT words No. 3326
272 Metanoia: Strong's NT words, No. 3341

translated as to *return*, or *turn around*. [273] At no point does it hint that God will *cause* repentance and 'do it to us'. In fact 'to cause repentance' is an oxymoron. Repentance is an act of the will, after which God relationally responds with an empowering to go farther. But at no point in repentance does He supersede the will. He would do so at the cost of the very meaning of repentance, obedience, response, and that for which we were created – relationship.

So what about this idea of being reconciled with God? Again, we find it is a relational process full of evidence of the need for choice.

If you were ready to be reconciled with someone who had seriously hurt you, would you be ready to acknowledge full reconciliation, even while they remained in hatred against you? Remember, we're not talking about forgiveness here. That can be given, even if the other party does not respond, but reconciliation is a two-way street.

True, God can state that He is reconciled with mankind through His gracious forgiveness. He can state that enough has been done to His satisfaction in *that* regard. But for reconciliation to bear its full fruit, it must grow into relationship. That, after all, is what Christ came to bring about; the restoration of a broken relationship.

So let's have a look at the essentials for real and full reconciliation. They are no less than you would expect in any reasonable relationship, and God is most reasonable.

First of all, the one who rebelled needs to be forgiven. By God's grace this forgiveness has been more than adequately provided.

"Blessed are they whose transgressions are forgiven, whose sins are covered. Blessed is the man whose sin the Lord will never count against him." [274] The good news is that we are already forgiven - all of us. That was expressed, once and for all, as the blood of Jesus flowed

---

273 Shuwb: Strong's OT words, No. 7725
274 Romans 4:7,8

from his broken heart. But remember, we're not just dealing with for-giveness here!

The second step toward reconciliation is that the selfish rebellion needs to stop. Stop it. Repent. Stop going in that selfish direction. Turn around.

True reconciliation continues with a realization that the results of the rebellion need to be remedied.

For this to take place two things must be added: a work of the re-deeming grace of God, and the obedient and continual response of the one being reconciled with God.

For His part, the Redeemer says, *"So I will restore to you the years that the swarming locust has eaten, You shall eat in plenty and be satisfied, And praise the name of the LORD your God, Who has dealt wondrously with you."* [275]

The Psalmist expected this at the time of his repentance when he wrote, *'Restore unto me the joy of thy salvation; and uphold me with thy free spirit.* [276]

In these ways God shows Himself to be enacting His part of the rec-onciliation. He is our Redeemer and Restorer, described by Peter in this way, *'And the God of all grace, who called you to his eternal glory in Christ, after you have suffered a little while, will himself restore you and make you strong, firm and steadfast. To him be the power for ever and ever. Amen.'* [277]

As for the rebel, there are definite steps for him to take. The first is to stop sinning, and God's powerful grace is available to all who choose to do so. Paul says, *'What shall we say, then? Shall we go on sinning so that grace may increase? By no means! We died to sin; how can*

---

275 Joel 2:25,26 NKJV
276 Psalm 51:12 KJV
277 1 Peter 5:10

we live in it any longer?...Therefore do not let sin reign in your mortal body so that you obey its evil desires.' [278]

After Repentance comes 'Restitution'.

This is seldom spoken of these days. I recall that one of the earliest stories I heard was of the Founder of The Salvation Army, William Booth, who testified that at the age of twelve he gave his life to God and was immediately convicted of the sin of theft. He had taken a silver pencil case from another boy and could not continue until he had humbled himself and returned the stolen property to its rightful owner. A childish story, perhaps, acted out by a mere boy. But it stuck with this mere boy after he heard it.

Making some act of restitution for our sins is an attempt to do what we can to defray the cost of our rebellion in the lives of those around us; those we have hurt. It is also a natural response of someone who realizes he has hurt the heart of the Father. It is nothing to do with winning our salvation. No act of ours can repay the full penalty of sin.

We are not talking about flagellating ourselves, or climbing on our knees the steep slopes to the Montserrat church, perched high on the rim of mountains that surround Bogotá, Colombia, as happens every year during Holy Week, when pilgrims make their painful ascent until the streets are red with their blood!

The price for our sins has been paid, once and for all. [279] Sufficient and efficacious blood has already been shed! We cannot add anything to the sacrifice already made, nor do we need to. It is more than adequate! In fact, it's positively prodigal! The writer of Hebrews continues, *'And where these have been forgiven, there is no longer any sacrifice for sin.'* [280]

---

278 Romans 6:1-12
279 Hebrews 10:10
280 Hebrews 10:18

Any acts of restitution we attempt are simply a natural love-response from those who have been forgiven. Zacchaeus leads the way, as Luke records, *"Look, Lord! Here and now I give half of my posses-sions to the poor, and if I have cheated anybody out of anything, I will pay back four times the amount."* [281] You'll notice Christ's response to this announcement, *"Today salvation has come to this house."* [282] He wasn't hinting that salvation comes through the act of penance, or by restitution. We might put it this way, *'Knowing this guy and his previous record I think we can safely say he has been converted. This has to be God!'*

However, a word to the wise; by delving back into your sinful past, in order try to put things right, can lead to some dramatic confronta-tions. It can do either the world of good, or a great deal of harm. Satan himself will happily remind you of how much harm you've done, and fill your itinerary for some years to come. Be led by the Spirit. Perhaps some acts of reconciliation can be made secretly, and - not that you need a reward – but, *'He who sees what is done in secret, will reward you.'* [283]

Reconciliation demands one more factor; the restored relationship needs to be maintained.

Is true reconciliation in place when one person in the relationship acts *'as a dog returning to its vomit?* [284] Is a broken marriage recon-ciled if, after a loving Second Honeymoon, the man returns to his mistress?

You will notice that in many of the steps toward reconciliation, our responses are called for. This is the walk of a disciple. The Christian life is a daily commitment to walk in God's ways. Every day Christ's disciples win victories right where the battle is fought, in the place of the will.

---

281 Luke 19:8
282 Luke 19:9
283 Matthew 6:4
284 Proverbs 26:11

As usual, the Psalmist says it best, *'I will walk about in freedom, for I have sought out your precepts.* [285] And, *'Teach me your way, O LORD, and I will walk in your truth; give me an undivided heart, that I may fear your name.'* [286]

---

285 Psalm 119:45
286 Psalm 86:11

20

Surrender, or Die!

IT IS WITH an ironic smile that we arrive at the conclusion that the ultimate choice, the moment of supreme victory for humanity over the great rebellion led by Satan, the moment when the light saber of truth strikes down the Darth Vader of the ages, comes about not when we rise up in supreme strength, but when we finally humble ourselves, and surrender to our Sovereign God.

Surrendering to God's sovereignty does not lead us back into a state of fatalism, but into moment-by-moment, day-by-day choices, to listen for Him, discern His desires, and to bring Him joy by walking obediently in His ways.

This is an active surrender, by which we respond out of our love and respect for our Maker, for the sheer joy and privilege of being alive, and being able to participate in God's high purposes.

Back to Psalm 86; *'I will surrender my will to Yours, Lord, so teach me Your ways and I promise to walk in Your truth. Help me, Lord, to have an undivided heart because I want to honor You and bring You glory by every choice I make.'*

Surrender is thought to be a weak response, but this surrender is a very strong choice. Paul said, *'At the name of Jesus every knee should bow, in heaven and on earth and under the earth, and every tongue confess that Jesus Christ is Lord, to the glory of God the Father.'* [287] There will indeed be a day when everything and everyone will bow the knee to the Lordship of Jesus. But, as the songwriter has said, *'Still the greatest treasure remains for those who gladly do it now'.* [288]

One of the great missteps of European history came when 'Christian' armies would defeat a pagan foe and the next thing would be to forcibly baptize the lot of them so that the victory over their culture was complete. After all, baptism by total emersion is a pretty effective way to force a decision. The victorious priest could always give the new 'convert' the option of being held under the water for a little longer than is generally recommended!

This error was repeated through the misguided zeal of some missionaries who declared whole tribes as having become 'Christian', whereas the truth was that possibly certain leaders had been converted. I recall the day when I asked a sophisticated native of a town in Kent whether or not she was a Christian. She glared at me, shocked at my question, and declared "Well! I *am* English!"

A similar response comes from Italian New Yorkers, (although when asked if they are Christian they often reply, "No, I'm Catholic!") But most of them would be hard pressed to discern between their Catholicism and their Italian culture. Giving up one would be tantamount to losing the other! And isn't this the position of so many kids who have grown up in Christian homes only to find themselves living the faith of their parents rather than the convictions of their own souls?

The victory of the ages doesn't come 'en masse' or community-wide. It comes one-by-one, as each individual sinner receives the light of the gospel through the revelation of the Holy Spirit, then repents of

287 Philippians 2:10,11
288 'Come, Now is the Time to Worship' by Brian Doerksen; Vineyard Songs

his foolish ways, bows his will to the Lordship of Jesus, and acknowledges Him as Lord of Heaven, of Earth, of all creation and of the will within his soul.

It was reported that Uri Gagarin, the first human to orbit the Earth, declared that he had not seen God out there. To be fair to Gagarin, it was later stated by Colonel Valentin Petrov, a close friend of Gagarin's, that the Cosmonaut had not said anything of the sort. The quotation, he claimed, was from none other than Nikita Khrushchev, speaking from the plenum of the Central Committee of the CPSU,[289] on the subject of anti-religious propaganda, where he said "Gagarin flew into space, but didn't see any god there!" It was later quipped from a Western source, that had Gagarin wanted to meet God, he need only have opened his hatch, and he would have found himself immediately in God's presence!

There will come a day when we will all stand before God to give an account of ourselves. Specifically we will be called to account for our deeds – what we have done. We will not be held accountable for what God has done, around us, to us, or through us. No-one will gain a crown of glory for being gifted by God's grace to preach, teach, draw the crowds, or heal the sick. Not one 'miracle worker' will be praised, save the One before whom the person stands. We will all be there by the work of grace on our lives, but we will be held accountable for how cheaply or lovingly we treated that grace.

Look at these verses. Can you spot the common ingredient in each statement?

'The Son of Man is going to come in his Father's glory with his angels, and then he will reward each person according to what he has done.'[290]

"But because of your stubbornness and your unrepentant heart, you are storing up wrath against yourself for the day of God's wrath,

---

289 The Communist Party of The Soviet Union
290 Matthew 16:27-28

when his righteous judgment will be revealed.
God "will give to each person according to what he has done." [291]
"Behold, I am coming soon! My reward is with me,
and I will give to everyone according to what he has done." [292]

The common denominator is that God will judge human-kind 'on that we have done'; our actions; the result of our choices. Would you expect a just judge to indict you for the sins of others? Of course not! How about being condemned for the sins of Adam? In the same way we should not expect to be judged for what God has done. It is clear that we will be held accountable for our own actions, our own choices.

This is no reward system based on our gifted contribution to society. That with which we were gifted was never our own. We will simply be judged for what we did with what we were given. The one with many gifts will stand alongside the one who had but a few. Both will be asked "What did you do with what I gave you?" The stories Jesus told about a master leaving his workers with a differing number of talents showed the master returning to judge their work. He did not praise the one for having been given much, or the other for having started with so little. The master returned to see what each had done with that with which he had been entrusted. [293]

If only we would catch hold of that fact. God does not look at how gifted we are. Our identity in His eyes is not based on what He has given us. His gifts are simply by grace – an *undeserved* favor. But He *will* take note of the choices we made, and how we used that which we were privileged to receive.

With that in mind, the greatly gifted should stand in the fear of the Lord and the lightly talented with something akin to relief! But let both recognize that it is how we have used our gifts that matters – to whose glory and to what end. Talented or otherwise, it is the result of our choices that will stand next to us on that day.

291 Romans 2:5,6
292 Revelation 22:12
293 Matthew 25:14-29

Let's leave the final speech to a leader of the ages, a man who knew what it was to choose rightly, to choose faithfulness over youthful foolishness, to choose humility in the face of popularity, and to choose personally rather than to run with the crowd. Joshua was a leader who knew the battle was waged not on the dusty plains of the Promised Land, but in the individual souls of his men. It was a battle over their choices. No more; no less.

Standing before the nation of Israel, just recently given him to lead, he declared, *"Now fear the Lord and serve him with all faithfulness. Throw away the gods your forefathers worshiped beyond the River and in Egypt, and serve the Lord. But if serving the Lord seems undesirable to you…."*

It was at this moment that Joshua challenged not only his hearers, the people of his generation, but every generation to come. His words have the ring of William Wallace, the Brave Heart of Scotland, as he stood to address his Celtic troops, facing the overwhelming odds of English might. As the clatter of English armor charged toward them across the open field, Wallace screamed "Hold! Hold! Hold!" But, for two hundred Highlanders to 'hold' that day, two hundred Highland hearts had to remain firm and prove themselves brave, one by one. Each man made an individual choice – to hold or to yield.

As for Joshua, he continued:

> *"Then choose for yourselves this day whom you will serve,*
> *whether the gods your forefathers served beyond the River, or the*
> *gods of the Amorites, in whose land you are living."*

Then he declared his choice!

> *"But as for me and my household, we will serve the Lord."*

Then the people answered, *"Far be it from us to forsake the Lord to serve other gods! It was the Lord our God himself who brought us and our fathers up out of Egypt, from that land of slavery, and performed those great signs before our eyes. He protected us on our entire journey and among all the nations through which we traveled. And the Lord drove out before us all the nations, including the Amorites, who lived in the land. We too will serve the Lord, because he is our God."*

Joshua pressed the point in an attempt to make it clear that hard choices lay ahead and that this was no fashion, fad, or cultural change to be adopted lightly. *"You are not able to serve the Lord. He is a holy God; he is a jealous God. He will not forgive your rebellion and your sins. If you forsake the Lord and serve foreign gods, he will turn and bring disaster on you and make an end of you, after he has been good to you."*

But the people said to Joshua, *"No! We will serve the Lord."* [294]

That was their choice. It is also mine. It can be yours.

Let the battle begin!

---

294 Joshua 24:14-21

CPSIA information can be obtained at www.ICGtesting.com
Printed in the USA
267949BV00001B/8/P